ISOTTA NOGAROLA'S
DEFENSE OF EVᴿ

A

De Pari aut In.

with Running \ ᵤₐ.ry and Commentary

THE EXPERRECTA SERIES

Women Latin Authors

Volume 1: The Passion of Perpetua
Volume 2: Isotta Nogarola's Defense of Eve

Series Editors:

Thomas G. Hendrickson
John T. Lanier
Anna C. Pisarello

pixeliapublishing.org

ISOTTA NOGAROLA'S DEFENSE OF EVE

A Latin Text of the

De Pari aut Impari Evae atque Adae Peccato

with Running Vocabulary and Commentary

Finn P. Boyle
Siria A. Chapman
Dhru Goud
Thomas G. Hendrickson
Siddhant Karmali
Kennedy Leininger
Justine A. Stern
Amelie Wilson-Bivera

PIXELIA PUBLISHING

Isotta Nogarola's Defense of Eve: A Latin Text of the *De Pari aut Impari Evae atque Adae Peccato* with Running Vocabulary and Commentary

First Edition

ISBN: 978-1-7370330-2-8

Published by Pixelia Publishing
pixeliapublishing.org

Cover design by Arhan Surapaneni
Cover photo: "Grayscale Photo of Dead Tree on Dry Land" published under a "free to use" CC0 license on Flickr
Font: Adobe Jenson Pro

CONTENTS

ACKNOWLEDGEMENTS

We would like to thank Stanford Online High School for providing the opportunity for the authors to produce this edition as part of an advanced Latin course. John Lanier, Anna Pisarello, and Ben Wiebracht, who are all teachers here, provided invaluable feedback and advice on the manuscript. Eli Gendreau-Distler (12th grade) wrote the code to aggregate our initial vocabulary list. Arhan Surapaneni (11th grade) designed our cover. Administrators Josh Carlson, Tomohiro Hoshi, and Christine Van Winkle provided logistical aid. More broadly, the supportive community at Stanford Online High School has fostered this project in countless ways.

We would also like to thank Margaret King, whose work on Isotta Nogarola has been not just an invaluable resource for us, but a source of inspiration as well. King's work is the foundation on which the present generation of scholarship about Nogarola has been built. Her work includes many articles on Nogarola, along with the *Isotta Nogarola: Complete Writings* edition co-edited with Diana Robin, to whom we are also grateful.

In addition, we would like to express our gratitude to several other people who provided inspiration for different aspects of the larger Experrecta series. Among the leaders in bringing to light Latin texts written by women, we would especially like to highlight the work of Laurie Churchill, Phyllis Brown, and Jane Jeffrey (Women Writing Latin); Joan Ferrante (epistolae.ctl.columbia.edu); Skye Shirley (skyeshirley.com); and Jane Stevenson (Women Latin Poets). Carlos Noreña provided a model for student-teacher co-publication in the humanities. Dickinson College Commentaries, Eleanor Arnold (latinteachertoolbox.com), Faenum Publishing, and Geoffrey

Steadman (geoffreysteadman.com) have led the way in offering open-access editions of Greek and Latin texts for students. Steadman has also kindly provided us advice and support.

Finally, we would like to thank the many friends and family members who helped us and supported us over the course of this last year. The gratitude expressed here can hardly convey the depth of our appreciation.

ABOUT THE EXPERRECTA SERIES

Women have written a substantial amount of Latin literature, but there are very few editions of that literature geared towards student use. The goal of the Experrecta series is to create student editions of Latin texts written by women. The aim of each edition is to assist students in reading the works of these authors in the original Latin. To that end, each edition will include help with the author's vocabulary and grammar, as well as an introduction to provide historical background on her life and works. The name of the series comes from Vibia Perpetua, who was among the first women to write a surviving work in Latin. In her narrative, Perpetua recounts a series of visions, each of which ends with the phrase *Et experrēcta sum* ("And I awoke"). This series will be populated by texts that have long been slumbering and are now waking to a new dawn and a new readership in Latin classrooms.

ABOUT THE AUTHORS

Joint authorship is uncommon in the humanities. A byline with eight names might well prompt questions, so we wanted to say a few words about our methods.

This book is the culmination of a project undertaken in an advanced Latin course at Stanford Online High School in the academic year 2021–2022. Hendrickson taught the course and organized the project. We divided the text into eight sections, and each of us (Boyle, Chapman, Goud, Hendrickson, Karmali, Leininger, Stern, and Wilson-Bivera) became the section editor for one portion of the text. As a first stage in the project, section editors edited and revised the on-page vocabulary, making sure that in each case we had the right word with the right definition. As a second stage, section editors checked the macrons in their portions of the text. The macrons had been added through a software program (alatius.com/macronizer) which was very effective but did need corrections. As a third stage, each section editor wrote a commentary for their section, deciding what needed to be explained in the Latin text and how to explain it. Section editors also provided peer review for each other after every stage of the project, and Hendrickson provided a final round of revisions. Hendrickson wrote the Introduction, which the students then revised in turn. Given this truly collaborative effort, a shared byline seemed the most appropriate way to describe the authorship of this edition.

INTRODUCTION

I. THE PURPOSE OF THIS EDITION

In 1451, Verona, Isotta Nogarola took up her pen in defense of Eve. For over a thousand years, writers from Tertullian to Boccaccio had blamed Eve for Original Sin: Eve had eaten from the tree of knowledge, and ever since then humans had inherited a sinful nature. In popular belief, Eve's sin was a consequence of women's inferiority and a justification for their subordinate role in society. Eve was foolish, weak-willed, and easily deceived. Her sin, moreover, was an act of defiance: an attempt to gain knowledge and power that had been forbidden to her.

Nogarola's *Defense of Eve*, which traditionally bears the title *Dē Parī aut Imparī Ēvae atque Ādae Peccātō*,[1] laid the foundation for an argument that women were not inherently inferior. As Margaret King and Diana Robin write, "The importance of this work and its place among inaugural texts in the history of the European controversy over gender and nature cannot be overstated" (2004: 142). Beyond that historical importance, the work is of high literary quality: Nogarola's writing is witty, ironic, and complex.

Despite the importance of Nogarola's *Defense of Eve*, there is no edition suitable for the Latin classroom. King and Robin have an English translation of the work in their 2004 *Isotta Nogarola: Complete Writings*, but the only modern edition of the Latin text is in Eugenius Abel's 1886 *Omnia Opera*, which provides the bare text

---

[1] This title (*On the Equal or Unequal Sin of Adam and Eve*) is the first line of a longer title, which we print in full on page 32. This is the title that Eugenius Abel chose for it in his 1886 critical edition, but each of the surviving manuscripts bears a different title. It is not clear which title, if any, goes back to Nogarola herself, and so we have taken the liberty of calling it by a new name, at least in English, the *Defense of Eve*, which we take from King's description of the work (1978: 818).

1

with no notes, grammatical help, or vocabulary aid.[2] The lack of an edition for students of Latin is particularly lamentable because the work provides students an opportunity to explore the cultural history of Latin. Nogarola could have written the work in her native Italian, and it is significant that she chose to write it in Latin instead.

Nogarola's choice of Latin positioned her as a figure of authority. In the first place, Nogarola's decision to use Latin signaled her participation in a debate with the scholastic theologians of the twelfth and thirteenth centuries. These theological works, which were written in a medieval form of Latin, still served as the basis for higher education in Nogarola's day. Nogarola responded to, and countered, the works of these theologians, who had seen Eve as bearing the primary guilt for sin. In addition, Nogarola's Latin also marked her as a figure in the world of Renaissance humanism, which flourished in Italy in the fourteenth and fifteenth centuries. The humanists of the Renaissance looked down on the Latin of the Middle Ages and sought to rediscover and reproduce the Classical Latin of ancient Rome. Nogarola was a humanist, and her eloquence in Classical Latin had already brought her fame. Nogarola's use of Latin was a humanist strategy to set herself up as an authoritative figure, in command of both the prestige language (Classical Latin) and the religious and literary authorities of the past, whom she quoted extensively.[3]

The primary goal of this edition is to allow students to engage directly with Nogarola's *Defense of Eve*, which is a work of fundamental importance for the history of gender and society. In addition, students will gain an introduction to scholasticism and humanism, and to the importance of these movements for the history of Latin.

---

[2] Abel's text of the *Defense of Eve* is at 1886: 2.187–216. Abel does provide a rich introduction to Nogarola and her works (1886: 1.i–clxxii), but given that the introduction is over a hundred pages long, and in Latin, it is likewise not well suited to the needs of students.

[3] For more detail on scholasticism, humanism, and Nogarola's use of Latin, see Introduction V–VI.

A secondary goal of this edition is to serve as a resource for scholars. Our Latin text builds on Abel's critical edition by incorporating readings from manuscripts to which he did not have access.[4] Moreover, Abel's edition provides no citations for the many quotations of prior authors embedded within the work. Many of these quotations have now been identified by King and Robin (2004), by Benckhuysen (2019: 30–35), and by Borelli, Buffon, and Jakubecki (2021). We have been able to build on the work of these scholars, identifying even more of the sources of the *Defense of Eve*.[5] There is still more work to be done both on the Latin text and on the quotations found within it, but such work would be beyond the scope of a student edition. For the present, this edition will have the most up-to-date Latin text and the most extensive commentary available on the Latin text and the sources of the *Defense of Eve*.

II. ISOTTA NOGAROLA, LUDOVICO FOSCARINI, AND THEIR DEBATE

Nogarola's *Defense of Eve* takes the form of a debate between herself and Ludovico Foscarini. The debate unfolded over the course of a series of letters, which Nogarola then edited for publication. The starting point of the debate was Augustine's claim that Adam and Eve "sinned unequally in respect to their sex, but equally in their pride" (*peccāvērunt imparī sexū sed parī fastū*).[6] Foscarini took the position that Eve's sin was greater, while Nogarola argued the greater sin was

---

[4] Introduction VII-VIII provides more detail on the textual history of the *Defense of Eve* and on the Latin text of this edition.

[5] The sources that we have newly identified can be found in chapters 2.1 (Augustine; Tertullian), 3.2 (Gregory the Great; Gratian), 3.5 (Sirach; Augustine), 3.9 (*Liber Dē Causīs;* Duns Scotus; Lucan), 3.13 (Gospel of John), 4.4 (Gregory the Great), 4.7 (Gratian), 4.8 (Julius Firmicus Maternus), 4.9 (*Liber Dē Causīs;* Duns Scotus), 4.10 (Augustine; Thomas Aquinas; Sirach), 5.4 (*Dīgesta;* Azo of Bologna), and 5.13 (Cicero).

[6] For more on this quotation and its context, see Introduction III.

3

Adam's. Though Nogarola and Foscarini were ostensibly debating the relative guilt of Adam and Eve, they used the controversy to explore gender, justice, free will, the search for knowledge, and the nature of sin.

Nogarola came into the debate with a formidable reputation.[7] Born around 1418, she struck out early for literary fame. Isotta's mother, Bianca, had provided a humanistic education for Isotta and her sisters. Humanism, which was a forerunner of the modern humanities, was an intellectual movement that focused on recovering the language, literature, and culture of ancient Rome. While still a teenager, Isotta, along with her sister Ginevra, exchanged letters with an expanding circle of humanist luminaries like Guarino da Verona. Epistolary exchanges were one of the main ways that humanists shared ideas and showed off their ability to produce eloquent Latin. Such letters were meant for public circulation, and humanists like Isotta used them to burnish their reputation. Nogarola did face detractors, one of whom circulated an anonymous invective alleging all sorts of sexual crimes,[8] but the scholarly community in general was largely welcoming and encouraging, if also condescending.[9] As she came to adulthood, Nogarola took the unusual path of avoiding both marriage and the convent, devoting herself instead to her studies.[10] At this time her focus of study also shifted, and she turned from the classical authors of ancient Rome to the study of Christianity.

---

[7] For more on the life and works of Isotta Nogarola, see especially Abel (1886: 1.i–clv), King (1994), Allen (2002: 944–69), King and Robin (2004), and Stevenson (2005: 156–65).

[8] For more on the anonymous pamphlet, see King and Robin (2004: 68–69) and Parker (2021). For the text of the pamphlet, see Segarizzi (1904: 50–54).

[9] On the general acceptance of the education of upper-class women, see Cox (2008: 11); on some examples of the encouraging, though condescending, attitude Nogarola faced, see King (1978).

[10] For more on Nogarola's decision not to marry, see King (1978) and King and Robin (2004: 101–107).

Ludovico Foscarini (1409–1480) met Nogarola when he was sent to govern Verona in 1451 on behalf of the Republic of Venice, which had conquered the city a generation earlier.[11] Foscarini had degrees in civil and canon law, and like Nogarola he had received a humanistic education as well. When Foscarini first arrived in Verona, Nogarola wrote him a letter of welcome, and the two struck up a friendship that over the years would become intense and complex.[12]

Our knowledge of their relationship is fragmentary because it relies on the intermittent survival of Foscarini's letters. Nogarola's letters to Foscarini unfortunately do not survive, apart from her letter of welcome and the letters that make up the *Defense of Eve*. In 1453, we find that the new bishop of Verona, Ermolao Barbaro the Elder, made Foscarini promise to stop seeing Nogarola.[13] After all, Foscarini was a married man and Nogarola an unmarried woman. In their cultural world, such a relationship was considered to be morally dangerous. Nevertheless, while Foscarini no longer visited Nogarola, their relationship continued through letters. An eight-year gap in the evidence ensues. Then in 1461 Nogarola's mother died. Foscarini wrote to a mutual friend and told him to send Nogarola to stay with him.[14] It appears that Nogarola was still there with Foscarini three years later: in a letter to Bishop Barbaro in 1464, Foscarini mentions in an off-hand way that Nogarola sends her greetings.[15]

The *Defense of Eve* seems to have grown out of conversations that Nogarola and Foscarini had been having when their relationship was still new. The genre of the work is unusual, perhaps unique. In one

---

[11] For more on Ludovico Foscarini, see King (1986: 374–77), King and Robin (2004: 114–37), and Bowd (2016).

[12] The letter of welcome is number LV in Abel's collection (1886: 2.28–34). For an overview of Nogarola's relationship with Foscarini, including an English translation of Letter LV, see King and Robin (2004: 114–37).

[13] The letter is number LVI in Abel's collection (1886: 2.35–38).

[14] The letter is number LXXXI in Abel's collection (1886: 2.159–60).

[15] The letter is number LXXXIV in Abel's collection (1886: 2.181–82).

sense, it is like a scholastic disputation.[16] Scholasticism was the intellectual movement that developed in medieval universities and used Latin disputations, or debates, to explore questions about philosophy and theology. The *Defense of Eve* resembles a scholastic disputation in that a central question is proposed and debated through arguments and rebuttals that rest sometimes on the citation of authorities and sometimes on logic. Yet the *Defense of Eve* takes the form of an epistolary exchange, a genre which, as mentioned above, was a favorite of the humanists.[17] Three of the early manuscripts of the work bear notes that claim Nogarola's letter of welcome to Foscarini prompted this debate-through-letters.[18] This claim might have been a conceit that originated with Nogarola and Foscarini themselves, though it might also be a supposition of the manuscript copyists. Although the work is a debate, Nogarola and Foscarini seem to be working with rather than against each other: a choreographed dance rather than fierce combat.

The work is suffused with irony. In order to establish that Eve was less guilty, Nogarola argues that women are inherently inferior in intellect and moral resolve, and therefore less responsible for their actions (2.1). In doing so, she highlights the "logical inconsistency of prevailing views about women… (since they) cannot be both the weaker sex by divine design and more culpable for original sin"

---

[16] On the history and nature of scholastic disputations, see Novikoff (2012).

[17] The *Defense of Eve* is frequently described by scholars as a dialogue, which is not the case. The idea of seeing the work as a dialogue goes back to Abel's critical edition of 1886, where he titles it a *dialogus* and formats the text as if it were a dialogue. Abel seems to have been influenced by the first print edition (1563), in which the work had been rewritten into a dialogue by Isotta Nogarola's grand-nephew Francesco. Yet it is clear both from the early manuscripts and from the text of the work itself that it was a written exchange with no pretense of speakers or the conventions of a dialogue. For more on the textual history of the *Defense of Eve*, see Introduction VII.

[18] It has been suggested that the *Defense of Eve* might be a written version of a debate that was held orally in public, but there is no evidence for such a debate.

(Benckhuysen 2019: 31).[19] Moreover, this argument puts Foscarini in the position of having to argue that women are not fundamentally inferior.

Nogarola also uses the work to make a defense against criticisms that were surely leveled against her as well as Eve. Foscarini argues that Eve's sin was greater because she sought knowledge beyond what was fit for her nature as a woman, which he characterizes as an act of arrogance (3.5). Nogarola, who spent her life seeking the kind of knowledge that was almost universally restricted to men, argues that the search for knowledge is not fueled by arrogance, but is rather an innate instinct for all humans (4.6).

III. EVE, MISOGYNY, AND THE HISTORY OF FEMINISM

Nogarola's work defending Eve marks an inflection point in the trajectory of the status of women in Europe.[20] Eve played an outsized role in how Christian communities thought about women. For over a thousand years, authors from Tertullian to Boccaccio had blamed Eve for the existence of sin.[21] Nogarola's rehabilitation of Eve built on, and argued against, this millennium-long tradition. At the same time, Nogarola's defense of women was a break with the past and the start of something new, now sometimes called "protofeminism," which began with the late-medieval author Christine de Pizan.[22] Nogarola

---

[19] This kind of irony is a tactic that Nogarola uses elsewhere with male interlocutors, as Boršić and Karasman (2015) argue.

[20] King and Rabil (2004) outline the cultural history of the status of women in ancient Greece and Rome, the Middle Ages, and the Early Modern period.

[21] Benckhuysen (2019: 15–22) surveys the history of the interpretation of Eve up until the Renaissance.

[22] Ferguson (2004: 7–9) outlines the notion of protofeminism; she points out that the term is useful for setting these early writers apart from the post-Enlightenment struggle for equality, but that the term is problematic because

was among the earliest, along with Christine de Pizan, to argue for women's inherent worth as humans, and the next few centuries saw many other writers following Nogarola and defending Eve.[23]

In the Book of Genesis (2–3), a snake convinces Eve to eat the fruit of the Tree of Knowledge, which had been forbidden by God. Eve, in turn, convinces Adam to eat as well. God punishes both with mortality and with expulsion from the Garden of Eden. Adam's particular punishment is to have to work for food, while Eve's is painful childbirth and subordination to her husband.

In Christian communities, the guilt of Eve came to be associated with all women. When the second-century author Tertullian wrote a two-volume work criticizing women for how they dressed, he started by asking them: "Don't you know that you are Eve?... You are the doorway to the devil, the unsealer of that notorious tree, the first to disobey divine law... on account of what you have earned, that is, death, even the son of God had to die" (*Dē Cultū Fēminārum* 1.1.1–2). This identification of all women with Eve would take on increased significance as a theology developed that posited that Christ came to the world in order to atone for original sin, and therefore it was Eve's fault that God had to be incarnated, suffer, and die on the cross. This accusation was influential and long-lasting: even in the *Defense of Eve* Nogarola takes pains to argue that it was Adam's actions, not Eve's, that ultimately resulted in the incarnation and death of Christ (2.4, 4.8).

Not all Christian writers saw Eve as solely or primarily responsible for sin. In the early fifth century, Augustine wrote that Adam and Eve sinned unequally in their sex but equally in their pride, which is the

---

it implies a single, linear history for feminism. Ferguson also (2004: 9–12) explores Christine de Pizan's place at the start of this tradition.

[23] Ardissino (2019: 283–95) surveys the history of works that, in the wake of the *Defense of Eve*, took up Eve's defense and argued on behalf of the dignity and value of women.

sentiment that Nogarola and Foscarini set as the starting point of their debate. The idea is present both in Augustine's *On the Literal Meaning of Genesis* 11.35 (*PL* 34.449) and in *City of God* 14.11–14. Augustine reasons that Adam and Eve each sinned through pride, both in their disobedience and in their unwillingness to take responsibility for their actions. In regard to how they sinned unequally in respect to their sex, Augustine argues that Eve, as a woman, was deceived by the serpent because she had less intelligence and resolve, while Adam was not deceived but made an active choice to follow Eve so that he would not be separated from her.

The question of Adam and Eve's relative guilt later became a topic of inquiry among the scholastic theologians of the twelfth and thirteenth centuries. Peter Lombard (1096–1160), in a chapter that engaged extensively with Augustine, concluded that Eve sinned more because she, unlike Adam, actually believed that she would be like God, and because she acted in the expectation that her sin would be forgiven (*Sententiae* 2.22). A generation later, Peter of Poitiers (1130–1215) revisited the question and likewise argued that Eve was more guilty (*Sententiae* 2.18). Finally, Thomas Aquinas (1225–1274) considered the question in his *Summa Theologica* (IIb Question 163 Article 4). Aquinas came to a three-part conclusion: 1) Adam bore greater responsibility for his sin in that he was more perfect than Eve; 2) they sinned equally in terms of the *genus* of sin because each sinned from pride; and 3) Eve sinned more greatly in terms of the *species* of sin because her pride was greater, because she caused Adam to sin, and because she did not sin out of love, as Adam had for her.

Nogarola and Foscarini engaged extensively with the arguments of the scholastic theologians. In fact, the opinion from Augustine that served as their starting point (*peccāvērunt imparī sexū sed parī fastū*, p. 32) is not a direct quotation of Augustine, but rather a paraphrase of Augustine from Peter of Poiters, which is emblematic of the extent

to which Nogarola and Foscarini were responding to the scholastic theologians more than to early Christian thinkers like Augustine.[24]

Despite the nuanced arguments about relative guilt in Thomas Aquinas, Eve continued to be seen as the guilty party in popular culture. Around 1361, Boccaccio wrote a collection of biographies of famous women, which started with a Life of Eve. Echoing arguments from the scholastics, Boccaccio wrote that because of her "womanly fickleness," she "foolishly believed" that she could be like God (*Dē Mulieribus Clārīs* 1.6).

And yet, things were beginning to change. Christine de Pizan wrote in defense of women in *Letter to the God of Love* (1399) and *The Book of the City of Ladies* (1405). In the *Letter*, she addressed the question of Eve specifically and argued both that Eve was not inferior and that Eve's guilt did not transfer to all women. Christine de Pizan's arguments sparked what later became known as the *querelle des femmes*, a debate that would foster arguments recognizing women's moral, intellectual, and spiritual equality with men.[25]

IV. ANTISEMITISM IN THE *DEFENSE OF EVE*

At several points in the *Defense of Eve*, Nogarola and Foscarini put forward arguments that are antisemitic.[26] In 3.13, Foscarini argues

---

[24] Borelli, Buffon, and Jakubecki (2021: 326) first realized that Nogarola and Foscarini found their quotation from Augustine in Peter of Poitiers, and they likewise found Nogarola and Foscarini to have almost exclusively taken their quotations of ancient authorities from medieval scholastic sources.

[25] For more on the *querelle des femmes*, see King and Rabil (2004: xix–xixx) and Ardissino (2019: 283–95).

[26] The term "anti-Jewish" is sometimes used rather than "antisemitic" to describe the Christian hostility to Jewish beliefs, practices, and people in the pre-modern world, since "antisemitism" connotes a type of racism, and Judaism had not yet been racialized. Yet the fifteenth century presents a gray area in this respect. Some Christians were beginning to view Jewish identity

that Jesus condemned the Jews as guiltier than Pilate on the grounds that their sin was prior to Pilate's, and so their sin caused his. In response (4.13), Nogarola writes that Jesus condemned the Jews not because their sin was first, but because they should have known better since, in her opinion, their scriptures clearly foretold Jesus's arrival. Finally, in 5.12, Foscarini argues that a number of factors show Pilate to be less guilty, such as the fact that he washed his hands of responsibility. Both Nogarola and Foscarini use the antisemitic epithet "the ignorant Jews" throughout these arguments. Despite their differing lines of reasoning, both Nogarola and Foscarini agree in taking for granted the idea that the Jewish people as a whole bear responsibility for the death of Jesus.

Antisemitism was pervasive in the Christian communities of fifteenth-century Europe. Nogarola and Foscarini were not unique in propagating antisemitic ideas; they, like most other Christians of the era, took these ideas for granted. Yet the pervasiveness of this antisemitism does not mean that it was therefore harmless. Arguments like those found in the *Defense of Eve* were used as the basis for a range of coercive and violent acts against Jews as the persecution of Jewish people intensified over the course of the early modern era. In 1492, all Jews would be expelled from Spain. In 1516, the Jews of Venice would be forced to live in a neighborhood called the "Ghetto," and this system of confinement soon spread to other cities. Almost everywhere, Jews faced increased legal restrictions and the risk of mob violence.

The antisemitic portions of the *Defense of Eve* will make uncomfortable reading for many students. Indeed, they should make for uncomfortable reading for us all. Yet we felt it was important not to excise these portions of the text or to otherwise side-step their

---

as something inherited and distinct from one's religious beliefs. Although each term ("anti-Jewish" and "antisemitic") is problematic when applied to this era, we have chosen to use "antisemitic" because the racializing of Judaism was already in progress.

11

problematic nature. Antisemitism was pervasive in Renaissance Italy in general and among humanists in particular, and this fact should not be elided or ignored.[27]

V. ANCIENT ROME, HUMANISM, AND THE HISTORY OF LATIN

The *Defense of Eve* is a enlightening text for Latin students because of the unique light it sheds on the history of Latin. Latin had been a written language for around two thousand years before Isotta Nogarola and the humanists. Yet the Latin language was never monolithic or static. Even in the earliest inscriptions, from the sixth to third centuries BCE, we find dialectical differences from one locality to another. A literary standard developed over the course of the second and first centuries BCE, but even then the language varied among the many different Latin-speaking communities which stretched across and beyond the Mediterranean and which contained millions of (often bilingual) speakers. As the centuries wore on, the spoken language changed more quickly than the written standard. The spoken form of Latin eventually became the various Romance languages (such as French, Spanish, Italian, and many others), but even then Latin itself kept a crucial place in various cultural spheres, like the Church and the University.

Latin textbooks and curricula today usually focus on one particular aspect of this multifaceted history: the "Classical Latin" found in literary works ranging from the second century BCE to the second century CE. The decision to focus on this phase of Latin in preference to all others is the legacy of a different era of Latin: Renaissance humanism.

---

[27] For more context on the history of humanism and antisemitism, see Bowd (2016), who focuses particular attention on Ludovico Foscarini.

The idea that there even is such a thing as "Classical Latin" is a notion that we owe to the humanists of the fourteenth and fifteenth centuries. Petrarch, along with other early humanists, argued that ancient Rome represented a zenith of language, literature, and human culture. They argued that there had followed a "Dark Age" in which all had languished, and that they were restoring the greatness ancient Rome. The humanists therefore studied the language and literature of ancient Rome, and they engaged with this material in hopes of improving their own society. The humanist era saw notable intellectual achievements: ancient Latin texts were rediscovered and the ancient Latin language came to be much better understood. A less fortunate byproduct of the era, however, was that it relegated all post-classical Latin to second-class status, including, ironically, the Latin writings of the Renaissance itself. The humanists, in effect, caused their own erasure.

Petrarch's trifold schema of history (from classical greatness to Dark Ages to Renaissance) is now roundly rejected within the academic world, even if it persists in some popular histories. The idea of a shining classical era that degenerated into medieval darkness has been replaced by histories that see the Middle Ages as a time of both continuity and transformation. In the case of literature, scholars have been increasingly exploring the richness of Latin in the medieval and early modern worlds on their own terms, rather than judging them by a set of anachronistic standards.

Yet Latin pedagogy has not caught up with Latin scholarship. There are relatively few student editions of medieval Latin texts, and only a handful for the Latin literature of the Renaissance and early modern eras, which is also called Neo-Latin.

By creating an edition of the *Defense of Eve*, we hope to provide students a window into a different era of Latin literature. The *Defense of Eve* is a humanist text to the extent that the authors generally use a classical standard for their Latin. At the same time, their usage was not rigid. As will be clear in the next section, Nogarola and Foscarini

freely took up late antique and medieval words and grammatical constructions when it suited their needs. Yet this too reflects a different aspect of humanism: the use of ancient language and literature to address issues in their own contemporary world. For them, the Latin language was not a museum piece, to be kept untouched for fear of mishandling. Rather, it was a tool that might get scuffed or bent out of shape, but which had a purpose and a power.

VI. THE LATIN OF THE *DEFENSE OF EVE*

The Renaissance humanists had a goal of restoring the grammar and style of Classical Latin. Accordingly, the Latin of Nogarola and Foscarini themselves will mostly accord with what students will have learned in introductory textbooks. However, Nogarola and Foscarini frequently quote texts from Late Antiquity and the Middle Ages, and these quotations often feature vocabulary, grammar, and stylistic features not commonly found in Classical Latin.[28] In addition, Nogarola and Foscarini occasionally use post-classical words and constructions, especially as they analyze and comment on these post-classical sources.

Nogarola and Foscarini quote extensively from late antique authors and works, like the Vulgate (fourth century),[29] Ambrose (fourth century),[30] Julius Firmicus Maternus (fourth century),[31] Hilary of Poitiers (fourth century),[32] Augustine (fourth/fifth century),[33] and

---

[28] For concise linguistic surveys of these eras of Latin, see Adams (2011) for Late Antiquity and Dinkova-Bruun (2011) for the Middle Ages.

[29] See 2.1, 2.2, 2.3, and throughout.

[30] See 4.4 and 4.6.

[31] See 4.8.

[32] See 4.8.

[33] See 2.1, 3.5, 4.6, 4.8, 4.9, 4.10, 5.12.

Gregory the Great (sixth century).[34] The Latin of this era, often called "Late Latin," had seen a number of changes from the Latin of Cicero's day. Among these late features, the most prominent in the *Defense of Eve* is the extended use of noun clauses beginning with *quod*. These *quod*-clauses gradually replaced the accusative-infinitive construction as a means of expressing indirect statement, and they could also be used for result clauses and indirect commands.[35]

Nogarola and Foscarini also engaged extensively, albeit usually tacitly, with authors and works from the later Middle Ages, like Peter Lombard (twelfth century),[36] Peter of Poitiers (twelfth century),[37] Gratian (twelfth century),[38] Bernard of Clairvaux (twelfth century),[39] Duns Scotus (thirteenth century),[40] and Thomas Aquinas (thirteenth century),[41] as well as medieval Latin translations of Aristotle and the *Liber Dē Causīs*, which was wrongly believed to be a work of Aristotle.[42] Indeed, as Borelli, Buffon, and Jakubecki (2021) have shown, even when Nogarola and Foscarini quote late antique sources, the phrasing of those quotations often shows that they were taken from the paraphrases of these later medieval authors.

These twelfth and thirteenth century authors were part of an intellectual movement now called scholasticism. These authors were scholars at the newly founded universities, and they wrote on theology, philosophy, and law. They developed a unique style of

---

[34] See 3.2, 3.12, 3.13, 4.4, 4.13, 5.12.

[35] See, e.g., 3.6 and 4.9.

[36] See 2.1.

[37] Quoted in the Latin title of the *Defense of Eve* (p. 32), see also Introduction III.

[38] See 3.2 and 4.7.

[39] See 4.9.

[40] See 3.9, 4.9, 5.8.

[41] See 3.2, 3.5, 4.4, 4.6, 4.7, 4.8, 4.9, 4.10.

[42] See 3.9, 4.9, 5.8.

medieval Latin, with its own idioms and technical grammar.[43] In the *Defense of Eve*, we find some scholastic features, especially in technical vocabulary, with phrases like *operātiō* ("action," 3.3 and 4.3), *vīsiōnis scientia* ("the knowledge of vision," referring to God's knowledge stemming from his ability to see the past and future, 4.7), *līberum arbitrium* ("free will," 4.9 and 5.9), *opposita* ("contrary propositions," 4.9) and *propter quod ūnumquodque tāle et illud magis* ("whatever makes a thing such as it is, is also that thing to an even higher degree," literally "on account of which thing each thing is such as it is, it is that thing even more," 3.9 and 4.9).

The *Defense of Eve* also exhibits grammatical forms commonly found in scholastic Latin. For instance, the ablative singular of comparative adjectives ends in -ī rather than -e (e.g. *dūriōrī poenā*, "with a harsher punishment," 1.1). Additionally, perfect passive verbs regularly use forms of "to be" in the perfect stem rather than in the imperfect stem (e.g. *fuit ausus* rather than *est ausus* for "he dared," 3.2).[44]

Finally, students may find it useful to know that Nogarola and Foscarini made use of some rhetorical structuring devices that, while classical, are much more common in scholastic Latin. For instance, they often recapitulate each others' arguments with a *quod*-clause containing a subjunctive of reported reason, as when Nogarola writes *Quod autem facilius potuerit amīcissima socia virum dēcipere quam turpissimus serpēns mulierem...* ("As to the fact that, according to you, a most loving partner could deceive her husband more easily than the most foul serpent could the woman," 4.11). Such a phrase is often followed with something to flag the start of one's own argument, like *dīcō*; in the case of the previous sentence, for instance, Nogarola continues with *multō minus peccāvit...dīcō* ("she sinned much less...I say," 4.11).

---

[43] For an introduction to scholastic Latin, see Schrader (2019).

[44] Auxiliaries in the perfect stem sometimes occurred in Classical Latin as well, especially in deponent verbs (see Pinkster 2015: 473–76), but the usage became far more common in the Middle Ages.

At the same time, Nogarola and Foscarini avoided the scholastic words and expressions that were most alien to Classical Latin, like *ly* as a definite article, or abstract nouns made from pronouns, like *quidditās* ("whatness").

VII. THE TEXTUAL HISTORY OF THE *DEFENSE OF EVE*

It is clear that Nogarola and Foscarini had a plan for Nogarola to join their writings together and disseminate them publicly as a unified work. Although they never specifically outline this plan, Foscarini seems to take it for granted in his final written response. At the start of that response he remarks that he will add a few arguments "so that you can sow the sweet seeds of paradise, so as to delight readers and light yourself up with glory" (5.1). Then at the very end of his response he comments that even if his thoughts are obscure, so long as his writings are joined to hers "they will be illuminated and shine in the darkness" (5.13).

The first readers of the *Defense of Eve* would probably have been members of Nogarola and Foscarini's social circle. Publication in the pre-print world essentially meant sharing a literary work with friends and acquaintances with the permission, and perhaps encouragement, that those friends make copies and share it out in turn. Two letters about the *Defense of Eve* survive from contemporaries within the world of Venetian humanism, and these provide evidence of this early circulation.[45] The work seems to have soon circulated more widely, and by the end of the fifteenth century it had reached readers far outside of Venice.

---

[45] One letter is from Matteo Bosso to Nogarola, numbered LXXVII in Abel's edition (1886: 2.127–32) and discussed by King and Robin (2004: 105–106); the other is an unpublished letter from Silvestro Lando to Nogarola (Hendrickson and Pisarello *forthcoming*).

The *Defense of Eve* received its *editiō princeps*, or first print edition, from the Aldine Press in 1563.[46] The printing was overseen by Isotta's grand-nephew Francesco Nogarola, who rewrote the text extensively. Francesco Nogarola changed the genre from an epistolary exchange to a Ciceronian-style dialogue, set in the gardens of Castel Azzano just outside Verona. Ludovico Foscarini was cut out entirely, and his arguments were redistributed to two new speakers: Leonardo Nogarola (Isotta's brother) and Giovanni Navagero (a governor of Verona in 1425). Giovanni Navagero was the ancestor of Cardinal Bernardo Navagero, who had just been made bishop of Verona in 1561. It seems that Francesco Nogarola rewrote and published the work as a way of honoring Navagero and welcoming him into the city.

The *editiō princeps* had a lasting influence on the reception of the work. It is probably due to the *editiō princeps* that the *Defense of Eve* is commonly referred to as a dialogue rather than as a scholastic disputation or an epistolary exchange. In addition, the *editiō princeps* did not print Nogarola's letter of welcome to Foscarini, which preceded the *Defense of Eve* in all known manuscripts. This deletion makes sense since Foscarini had been cut from the dialogue, but it seems that the letter should be considered part of the original work.

The only modern edition of the Latin text of the *Defense of Eve* is the one made in 1886 by Eugenius Abel, who edited the complete works of Isotta Nogarola along with those of her sister Ginevra and aunt Angela. Abel's edition is extremely careful, and it is remarkable what he was able to achieve given his circumstances. At the same time, his Latin text suffered both from his limited access to the manuscripts and from his method in selecting readings. A new critical edition of the *Defense of Eve* is needed, one in which the text is totally reconstituted based on new readings from all the now-known manuscripts, but such a project would be outside of the scope of a

---

[46] For more on the *editiō princeps*, see Abel (1886: 1.li–lv) and Boršić and Karasman (2015: 47–49). For the text of the *editiō princeps*, see Abel (1886: 2.219–57).

student reader. Two of the co-editors of the Experrecta Series (Hendrickson and Pisarello) are working on a new critical edition, and we have been able to incorporate into this present edition some of their improvements and corrections to Abel's text (see Table 1).

Table 1[47]

Abel's Edition	Pixelia Edition
D. D. (187) V	dominum (in title) N
Lodovicus incipit (187) V	Prōpositiō Lodovīcī (1.1) F[48]
nostrī[49] (187)	tamen (1.1) FLNCV
Isōta (188) VN	Rēspōnsiō Isōtae (2.1) F
Lodovīcus (192) VN	Rēspōnsiō Lodovīcī (3.1) F
Isōta (197) VN	Rēspōnsiō Isōtae (4.1) F
Parī enim gressū (199) C	Parī etiam gressū (4.3) N
Fragilitās autem (201) C	Fragilitās etiam (4.6) FLN
sed quod (203) C	secundum quod (4.6) N
Psalmō LXIIII (206) NC	Psalmō LXVIII (4.8) FL
omnis et Ādae (206) C	omnis etiam Ādae (4.9) FLN
causae[50] causātī (206)	causa causātī (4.9) FLNC
hīs (206) C	iīs (4.9) FLN
Lodovīcus (211) VN	Rēspōnsiō Lodovīcī et Conclūsiō Quaestiōnis (5.1) F

---

[47] In Table 1, the page number is provided for the readings in Abel's edition and the corresponding chapter number for this Pixelia edition. After the page or chapter number, we also indicate the manuscript that is the basis for the reading. The full information for these manuscripts (F, L, N, C, and V) can be found in the bibliography.

[48] Manuscripts L and C have similar designations that mark each time there is a change between the writing of Nogarola and Foscarini.

[49] Abel's apparatus criticus suggests that *nostrī* is the reading C, but this appears to be a mistake on the part of Abel or whoever copied the readings of C for him. C has the abbreviation *tn*, which is short for *tamen* but might have been mistaken for an abbreviation for *nostrī*.

[50] The *causae* (rather than *causa*) here is not based on any manuscript and appears to be a rare typo in Abel's edition.

immō (211) C
hīs (212) LVC
quum (212) C
contrā lēgēs (212) V
Ūnus (215) CV

ideō (5.2) FLN
iīs (5.3) FN
quoniam NLV
contrā nātūrae lēgēs (5.4) FLNC
Vīvis (5.13) FLN

VIII. ABOUT THIS EDITION: RATIONALE OF THE LATIN TEXT, VOCABULARY, AND COMMENTARY

In addition to the changes to the Latin text outlined above in Table 1, we also changed the punctuation and paragraphing, and we added chapter divisions in order to clarify the organization of the arguments and ease cross-reference (see Introduction IX). We keep Abel's page numbers, which we place in [square brackets] in the text.

We also made a few orthographical changes to the Latin text for the ease of students. For instance, Abel's text uses forms like *quum* and *loquūtus*, while we use the more easily recognizable spellings *cum* and *locūtus*. We also added macrons to the text. Since Nogarola and Foscarini did not use macrons, which had not yet been developed as a way to mark long vowels, this change requires a word of explanation.

We have decided to include macrons primarily because they make the Latin easier to read by distinguishing forms that would otherwise be identical (e.g. *poenā* and *poena*). In addition, macrons help to better represent the sounds of the Latin language, and so they are of particular help to students as they learn to *read* Latin— that is, to say or think the Latin words and understand them, rather than looking at the Latin words and trying to remember their English equivalents.

While it is true that ancient Roman texts did not include macrons, it is worth noting that they likewise did not include lowercase letters

and punctuation— at least of the sort that modern texts employ.[51] Yet we use lowercase letters and modern punctuation because they make Latin texts easier to read, and the same rationale should apply to macrons.

The use of macrons is admittedly more dubious for a fifteenth-century Latin text than it is for an ancient Latin text. The pronunciation of Latin had changed considerably: Nogarola and Foscarini would have pronounced Latin in the same way that they pronounced their Italian, which means that these macrons did not represent the sounds of Latin as they spoke it. All the same, as humanists, they were *trying* to use Latin as it would have been in ancient Rome, and so it still seems reasonable to apply an orthographic practice that accords with a classical standard.

For the on-page vocabulary, since there would not be room on the page to gloss all words, our goal was to provide definitions for the words that students would be least likely to know and put all other words in a glossary at the back of the book. As a criterion, which is admittedly arbitrary, we settled for moving to the back of the book the 250 most common words in the Latin language, according to the Dickinson College Commentaries Core Vocabulary List. Apart from those words, we also moved to the back a few words that occur on almost every page: "Adam" (Ādam, Ādae m.), "Eve" (Ēva, Ēvae f.), "woman" (mulier, mulieris f.), and "sin" (both as a verb, peccō [1], and a noun, peccātum, peccātī n.).

For the commentary, our primary goal was to explain the Latin, with a particular view to issues that might cause trouble for students. The limited space on the page means that little room was left to comment

---

[51] Romans did employ cursive scripts, especially in informal documents, and they likewise had some punctuation marks, though not modern ones like commas and periods. Latin texts of the fifteenth century did employ some distinct majuscule and minuscule letters, as well as a kind of punctuation, but these too do not follow the same rationale and use as modern texts.

on any other aspects of the work, though we did try to cite the sources that Nogarola and Foscarini drew on, in particular because we have been able to identify more of these sources than previous editions have.

IX. CHAPTER SUMMARY OF THE *DEFENSE OF EVE*

The arguments in the *Defense of Eve* can be hard to follow because they proceed in a rapid, almost staccato fashion. Yet there is a logic to the organization, and the arguments mirror each other in a careful symmetry from one section to the next.

In order to make clear the structure and logic of the piece, we have added chapter divisions and subdivisions. Each of the five written statements, which seem to have originally been letters, is here treated as a chapter: so the first chapter is Foscarini's proposition, the second chapter is Nogarola's response, and so on. Within each chapter, we have made subdivisions to separate out the various arguments within that chapter (2.1, 2.2, etc.). We also keep Abel's page numbers, which we place in [square brackets] in the Latin text. An outline of the whole is as follows:

1. Foscarini's proposition: Eve is more guilty than Adam
1.1 Foscarini provides four reasons why Eve is more guilty than Adam: she received a harsher penalty from a fair judge (God); she committed the possibly-unforgivable sin of wanting to become like God; she was the first cause of sin, and so responsible for all subsequent sins; Adam is less guilty because was led into sin by a loved one

2. Nogarola's response: Eve is less guilty than Adam
2.1 Opening pleasantries; argument that Eve's ignorance and inconstancy mean that she bears less responsibility
2.2 Adam disobeyed a direct command from God, therefore he sinned more

2.3 Response to Foscarini's argument (1.1) that Eve wanted to become like God: rather, she was simply weak and prone to indulgence

2.4 Response to Foscarini's argument (1.1) that Eve was the first cause of sin: Adam's sin was more consequential for future generations

2.5 Response to Foscarini's argument (1.1) that Eve suffered a harsher penalty: Adam's penalty (death) was worse than Eve's

2.6 Closing pleasantries

3. Foscarini responds to Nogarola's arguments and offers new arguments to support his own points

3.1 Opening pleasantries

3.2 Response to Nogarola's argument (2.1) that Eve's ignorance makes her less responsible: sinning from ignorance is worse, and God made Eve's intellect

3.3 Response to Nogarola's argument (2.1) that Eve's inconstancy makes her less responsible: sinning from inconstancy is worse

3.4 Adam's guardianship does not excuse Eve[52]

3.5 Response to Nogarola's argument (2.3) that Eve sinned out of weakness: Eve sinned out of arrogance because she desired more knowledge than was fit for her

3.6 Response to Nogarola's argument (2.4) that Adam's sin was more consequential: Eve's sin might have been unforgivable, like the devil's, whereas Adam's sin brought about the coming of Christ

3.7 Response to Nogarola's response (2.5) to Foscarini's argument (1.1) that Eve received a harsher penalty: Eve received all of Adam's punishments, and more in addition

3.8 Foscarini pivots from rebuttals to offering his own positive arguments

3.9 Argument that Eve caused Adam to sin

---

[52] Foscarini implicitly suggests that Nogarola has argued that Adam's guardianship excuses Eve, yet Nogarola has not voiced such an argument. It might be the case that the argument was later removed by Nogarola and Foscarini.

3.10 Argument that since Eve was inferior to Adam, she attempted a greater rise in station than Adam by trying to become like God, and therefore committed the greater sin

3.11 Argument that a loving wife can deceive a husband more easily than a foul serpent should be able to deceive a woman

3.12 Argument that Eve sinned for longer, and therefore sinned more

3.13 Argument that Eve's sin was worse because it was first: an antisemitic argument that Jesus condemned the Jewish people as more guilty than Pilate

3.14 Closing pleasantries

4. Nogarola responds to Foscarini's responses and new arguments

4.1 Opening pleasantries

4.2 Response to Foscarini's response (3.2) to Nogarola's argument (2.1) about Eve's ignorance: Eve's ignorance does excuse her because it is innate

4.3 Response to Foscarini's response (3.3) to Nogarola's argument (2.1) about inconstancy: Eve's inconstancy also excuses her because it is also innate

4.4 Response to an argument about imperfection[53]: Adam was complete, but Eve simply existed to further Adam's happiness

4.5 Response to Foscarini's argument (3.4) about guardianship: divine law treats the matter differently from secular law

4.6 Response to Foscarini's argument (3.5) that Eve sinned from arrogance: the desire for knowledge is natural, and it is more arrogant to disobey God's command

4.7 Response to Foscarini's response (3.6) to Nogarola's argument (2.4) that Adam's sin was more consequential: Eve's sin differed from the devil's because she wanted knowledge, not power, and because she expected forgiveness

---

[53] Nogarola here implicitly suggests that Foscarini has made an argument about Eve's imperfection, yet Foscarini has not voiced such an argument. As above (3.4), it might be the case that the argument was later removed by Nogarola and Foscarini.

4.8 Response to Foscarini's response (3.7) to Nogarola's response (2.5) to Foscarini's argument (1.1) that Eve suffered a harsher penalty: Adam's penalty was harsher, since it required Christ's death to redeem it

4.9 Response to Foscarini's arguments (3.9) about Eve as the first cause of sin: if Adam had free will, then he (not Eve) is responsible for his sin

4.10 Response to Foscarini's argument (3.10) that Eve's inferior status made the sin of arrogance worse: only a superior can force someone to do something, but Eve was inferior to Adam

4.11 Response to Foscarini's argument (3.11) that a loving wife can deceive a husband more easily than a foul serpent should be able to deceive a woman: Eve (ignorant) was persuaded by the (wise) serpent; Adam (wise) should not have been persuaded by his (ignorant) wife

4.12 Response to Foscarini's argument (3.12) that Eve sinned more greatly because she sinned for a longer time: this is negated by the fact that Adam and Eve were not equals

4.13 Response to Foscarini's argument (3.13) that Eve's sin was worse because it was first: an antisemitic argument that Jesus condemned the Jewish people not because they first condemned him, but because they had reason to know better

4.14 Closing pleasantries

5. Foscarini's final response

5.1 Opening pleasantries

5.2 Response to Nogarola's response (4.2) to Foscarini's response (3.2) to Nogarola's argument (2.1) that Eve's ignorance excuses her: her ignorance was not innate but willful because she chose to trust the serpent over God

5.3 Response to Nogarola's response (4.3) to Foscarini's response (3.3) to Nogarola's argument (3.2) that Eve's inconstancy excuses her: God gave her suitable character and nature to attain salvation

5.4 Response to Nogarola's response (4.4) to an argument about Eve's imperfection: if Eve was created to help Adam, she acted contrary to what she ought to have done

5.5 Response to Nogarola's argument (4.6 and 2.2) that transgression is the greater sin: Adam's transgression of God's command is not relevant, because Eve transgressed it as well

5.6 Response to Nogarola's response (4.7) about the difference between Eve's sin and the devil's, which responded to Foscarini's response (3.6) to Nogarola's argument (2.4) that Adam's sin was more consequential: the difference between the sin of angels and man is too big a topic to discuss here

5.7 Response to Nogarola's response (4.8) to Foscarini's response (3.7) to Nogarola's response (2.5) to Foscarini's argument (1.1) that Eve's punishment was harsher

5.8 Response to Nogarola's response (4.9) to Foscarini's argument (3.9) to Eve caused Adam to sin: Foscarini rejects Nogarola's interpretation of Aristotle

5.9 Response to Nogarola's response (4.10) to Foscarini's argument (3.10) about Eve's inferiority: Foscarini acknowledges that Adam had free will and that the fault does not entirely rest with Eve

5.10 Response to Nogarola's response (4.11) to Foscarini's argument (3.11) that a wife can deceive a husband more easily than a foul serpent should be able to deceive a woman: women are deceptive

5.11 A (loosely connected) response to Nogarola's response (4.12) to Foscarini's argument (3.12) that the longer a sin goes on, the graver it is: Eve's sin is greater than Adam's because we have not yet found a way to heal it

5.12 A response to Nogarola's response (4.13) to Foscarini's argument (3.12) about Pilate and the Jews: Foscarini claims various elements of support from the gospels

5.13 Closing pleasantries

BIBLIOGRAPHY

Manuscripts:

F: Florentinus (Biblioteca Nazionale Centrale di Firenze)
   Magliabecchianus XXXVIII 142
L: Laurentianus (Biblioteca Lorenziana) 90 sup. 47
N: Neapolitanus (Biblioteca Nazionale di Napoli) V B 35
V: Veronensis (Biblioteca Capitolare) 256
C: Corsinianus (Biblioteca dell'Accademia Nazionale dei Lincei e
   Corsiniana) 839 (43 D 8)

Editions:

Abel, Eugenius, ed. 1886. *Isotae Nogarolae Veronensis opera quae
   supersunt omnia, accedunt Angelae et Zeneverae Nogarolae
   epistolae et carmina.* 2 vols. Gerold.
King, Margaret L. and Diana Robin, eds. and trans. 2004. *Isotta
   Nogarola: Complete Writings. Letterbook, Dialogue on Adam
   and Eve, Orations.* University of Chicago Press.
Nogarola, Francesco, ed. 1563. *Isotae Nogarolae veronensis,
   dialogus, quo, utrum Adam vel Eva magis peccaverit, quaestio
   satis nota, sed non adeo explicata, continetur.* Aldine Press.

Studies:

Adams, J. N. 2011. "Late Latin," in J. Clackson, ed., *A Companion
   to the Latin Language*, 257–283. Wiley-Blackwell.
Allen, Prudence. 2002. *The Concept of Woman. Vol. 2: The Early
   Humanist Reformation, 1250–1500.* Eerdmans.
Ardissino, Erminia. 2019. "Women Interpreting Genesis in Early
   Modern Italy: Arguments Supporting Gender Equality," in E.

Ardissino and E. Boillet, eds., *Lay Readings of the Bible in Early Modern Europe*, 276–296. Brill.

Benckhuysen, Amanda W. 2019. *The Gospel According to Eve: A History of Women's Interpretation*. InterVarsity Press.

Borelli, Marcela, Valeria A. Buffon, and Natalia G. Jakubecki. 2021. "The Fruit of Knowledge: To Bite or Not to Bite? Isotta Nogarola on Eve's Sin and its Scholastic Sources," in *Women's Perspectives on Ancient and Medieval Philosophy*, ed. I. Chouinard, Z. McConaughey, A. Madeiros Ramos, and R. Noël, 321–341. Springer.

Boršić, Luka and Ivana Skuhala Karasman. 2015. "Isotta Nogarola— The Beginning of Gender Equality in Europe." *The Monist* 98: 43–52.

Bowd, Stephen. 2016. "Civic Piety and Patriotism: Patrician Humanists and Jews in Venice and its Empire." *Renaissance Quarterly* 69: 1257–1295.

Cox, Virginia. 2008. *Women's Writing in Italy, 1400–1650*. Johns Hopkins University Press.

Dinkova-Bruun, Greti. 2011. "Medieval Latin," in J. Clackson, ed., *A Companion to the Latin Language*, 284–302. Wiley-Blackwell.

Ferguson, Margaret W. 2004. "Feminism in Time." *Modern Language Quarterly* 65: 7–27.

Hendrickson, Thomas G. and Anna C. Pisarello. (forthcoming). "An Unpublished Letter to Isotta Nogarola from Silvestro Lando."

King, Margaret L. 1978. "The Religious Retreat of Isotta Nogarola (1418–1466): Sexism and Its Consequences in the Fifteenth Century." *Signs* 3: 807–822.

King, Margaret L. 1986. *Venetian Humanism in an Age of Patrician Dominance*. Princeton University Press.

King, Margaret L. 1994. "Isotta Nogarola," in *Italian Women Writers: A Bio-Bibliographical Sourcebook*, ed. Rinaldina Russell, 313–323. Greenwood Press.

King, Margaret L. and Albert Rabil Jr. 2004. "The Other Voice in Early Modern Europe: Introduction to the Series," in M. L.

King and D. Robin, eds., *Isotta Nogarola: Complete Writings. Letterbook, Dialogue on Adam and Eve, Orations*, xi–xxxi. University of Chicago Press.

Novikoff, Alex J. 2012. "Toward a Cultural History of Scholastic Disputation." *American Historical Review* 117: 331–364.

Parker, Josey. 2021. "How to be a Classical Scholar—and a Woman—in the Fifteenth Century." *Antigone Journal* https://antigonejournal.com/2021/03/isotta-nogarola/ (Last Accessed Jan. 26, 2022)

Pinkster, Harm. 2015. *The Oxford Latin Syntax. Volume I: The Simple Clause.* Oxford University Press.

Schrader, Dylan. 2019. *The Shortcut to Scholastic Latin.* Paideia Press.

Segarizzi, Arnaldo. 1904. "Niccolò Barbo, patrizio veneziano del secolo XV, e le accuse contro Isotta Nogarola." *Giornale storico della letteratura italiana* 43: 39–54.

Stevenson, Jane. 2005. *Women Latin Poets. Language, Gender, and Authority from Antiquity to the Eighteenth Century.* Oxford University Press.

Abbreviations

abl.	ablative
acc.	accusative
adj.	adjective
adv.	adverb
cf.	compare to (*cōnfer*)
CL	Classical Latin
comp.	comparative
dat.	dative
e.g.	for example (*exemplī grātiā*)
etc.	and the rest (*et cētera*)
fem.	feminine
fut.	future
gen.	genitive
inf.	infinitive
masc.	masculine
neut.	neuter
nom.	nominative
pass.	passive
perf.	perfect
pl.	plural
PL	*Patrologia Latina*
prep.	preposition
sg.	singular
subj.	subjunctive
[]	square brackets indicate the pagination of Abel's 1886 edition

Dē Parī aut Imparī Ēvae atque Ādae Peccātō
with Running Vocabulary and Commentary

Dē Parī aut Imparī Ēvae atque Ādae Peccātō

DĒ PARĪ AUT IMPARĪ ĒVAE ATQUE ĀDAE PECCĀTŌ,

PRAECLĀRA INTER CLĀRISSIMUM DOMINUM LODOVĪCUM

FOSCARĒNUM, VENETUM, ARTIUM ET UTRIUSQUE IŪRIS DOCTŌREM,

ET GENERŌSAM AC DOCTISSIMAM DĪVĪNAMQUE DOMINAM ISŌTAM

NOGARŌLAM, VĒRŌNĒNSEM, CONTENTIŌ

SUPER AURĒLĪ AUGUSTĪNĪ SENTENTIAM, VIDĒLICET:

PECCĀVĒRUNT IMPARĪ SEXŪ SED PARĪ FASTŪ.

---

ars, artis f.: art
Augustīnus, -ī m.: Augustine
Aurēlius, -ī m.: Aurelius
clārus, -a, -um: bright; famous
contentiō, -ōnis f.: contention; dispute
doctor, -ōris m.: teacher; expert
doctus, -a, -um: erudite
domina, -ae f.: lady
dīvīnus, -a, -um: divine
fastus, -ūs m.: arrogance
Foscarēnus, -ī m.: Foscarini
generōsus, -a, -um: noble
impār, imparis: unequal
Isōta, -ae f.: Isotta

iūs, iūris n.: law
Lodovīcus, -ī m.: Ludovico
Nogarōla, -ae f.: Nogarola
pār, paris: equal
praeclārus, -a, -um: very bright; very
famous
sententia, -ae f.: opinion
sexus, -ūs m.: sex (biological)
super (+ acc.): over; on
uterque, utraque, utrumque: both
Venetus, -a, -um: Venetian
Vērōnēnsis, -e: from Verona
vidēlicet: namely; specifically

---

praeclāra...contentiō: *the famous...dispute;* the widely separated adjective and noun
bracket the names of those involved; these seven lines are the traditional title

Lodovīcum Foscarēnum: *Ludovico Foscarini;* a Venetian aristocrat

artium et utriusque iūris doctōrem: *doctor of the arts and of both kinds of law;* that is,
civil law and canon law; Foscarini received his Doctorate of Arts degree from the
University of Padua in 1429 and his Doctorate of Law there in 1434

doctissimam dīvīnamque...Isōtam Nogarōlam: *the very erudite and divine Isotta
Nogarola;* from a noble family in Verona, Nogarola had a reputation as a scholar and,
after choosing not to marry, a reputation as a holy woman

Aurēlī Augustīnī sententiam: *the opinion of Aurelius Augustine;* Augustine writes similar
ideas in *City of God* 14.14 and *On the Literal Meaning of Genesis* 11.35 (*PL* 34.449),
but this formulation of the idea is from the scholastic author Peter of Poitiers *Sent.* 2
ch. 18 (see Introduction III)

1.1 Prōpositiō Lodovīcī: Sī qua tamen peccātī gravitās maior esse potest, Ēva damnābilior fuit, quia ā iūstō iūdice dūriōrī poenā damnāta, quia Deī sē similem fierī magis crēdidit, quod ad speciēs irremissibilium peccātōrum [188] in Spīritum Sānctum accēdit, quia suggessit et fuit causa peccātī Ādae, nōn ē contrā, item quia, licet turpis sit excūsātiō amīcī causā peccāre,

accēdō, -ere, accessī, accessum: to come near, approach
aliquī, aliqua, aliquod: some, any
contrā: to the contrary (adv.)
damnābilis, -e: worthy of condemnation
damnō (1): to condemn
excūsātiō, -ōnis f.: excuse
gravitās, -tātis f.: weight; gravity
irremissibilis, -e: unforgivable
item: likewise
iūdex, iūdicis m.: judge
iūstus, -a, -um: just, fair

licet (+ subj.): although
Lodovīcus, -ī m.: Ludovico (Foscarini)
maior, maius: greater (comp. adj.)
prōpositiō, -ōnis f.: proposition
sānctus, -a, -um: sacred, holy
similis, -e (+ gen. or dat.): like, similar to
speciēs, speciēī f.: appearance; type
spīritus, -ūs m.: spirit
suggerō, suggerere, suggessī, suggestum: to suggest
turpis, turpe: ugly; disgraceful

Sī (ali)qua...gravitās: *If any...seriousness;* the *ali-* is left out of *aliquī* after *sī, nisi, num,* and *nē*
tamen: *nevertheless;* this word looks back to Augustine's opinion that Adam and Eve sinned equally in pride
quia ā iūstō...quia Deī...quia suggessit...item quia: Ludovico puts forward four reasons why he believes Eve is more worthy of blame
ā iūstō iūdice: *by a just judge;* God
dūriōrī poenā damnāta (est): *(she was) condemned to a harsher penalty;* the subject is Eve; *dūriōrī* is a post-classical form of the abl./sg./fem. (= CL *dūriōre*)
quod ad speciēs...accēdit: *which approaches the class of unforgivable sins;* the antecedent of this *quod* is the entire preceding clause (the idea of making oneself more similar to God)
in Spīritum Sānctum: *against the Holy Spirit*
amīcī causā: *because of a friend;* the abl. *causā* + gen. is an idiom

nūlla tamen tolerābilior quā ductus est Ādam.

2.1 Rēspōnsiō Isōtae: Mihi autem, postquam mē prōvocās, longē aliter contrāque vidētur; nam ubi minor sēnsus minorque cōnstantia, ibi minus peccātum; et hoc in Ēvā, ergō minus peccāvit. Unde hoc cognōscēns serpēns ille callidus initium tentātiōnis sūmpsit ā fēminā, dubitāns quidem hominem propter cōnstantiam

---

aliter: otherwise, differently
callidus, -a, -um: crafty
cognōscō, -ere, cognōvī, cognitum: to recognize
cōnstantia, -ae f.: constancy; strong character
contrā: to the contrary (adv.)
dubitō (1): to doubt; hesitate
fēmina, -ae f.: woman
ibi: there
initium, -ī n.: beginning, start
Isōta, -ae f.: Isotta (Nogarola)
longē: a long way; by far (adv.)
minor, minus: less (adj.)

minus: less (adv.)
postquam: after; because
propter (+ acc.): on account of
prōvocō (1): to call out; challenge
rēspōnsiō, -ōnis f.: response
sēnsus, -ūs m.: sense, mental capacity
serpēns, serpentis m.: snake
sūmō, -ere, sūmpsī, sūmptum: to take up; begin
tentātiō, -ōnis f.: temptation; trial
tolerābilis, -e: tolerable
unde: from where; from which thing; that's why

---

nūlla tamen (excūsātiō est): *yet no (excuse is);* "excuse" is implicit from previous clause
tolerābilior quā: *more tolerable (than the one) by which;* there is an implicit antecedent in an abl. of comparison; the *quā* is abl. of means
ductus est Ādam: *Adam was led (into sin);* Foscarini will clarify later (3.11) that this point contrasts with Eve, who was led into sin by the serpent
minus peccāvit: *she sinned less;* the *minus* here is an adverb
dubitāns...hominem...nōn posse superārī: *doubting (on the grounds that) the man could not be overcome;* the verb *dubitāre* here has a sense of "to doubt" or "hesitate," and it sets up an indirect statement giving the reasoning of the one in doubt; the statement is a paraphrase of a sentence from Augustine *City of God* 14.11, and a version of the idea goes back to Tertullian *Dē Cultū Fēminārum* 1.1.2

nōn posse superārī. *Sententiārum* II.°: Stāns cōram fēminā, hostis antīquus nōn est ausus in verba persuāsiōnis prōrumpere, sed sub interrogātiōne eam alloquitur: "Cūr praecēpit vōbīs Deus nē comederētis dē lignō paradīsī?" At illa: "Nē forte moriāmur." Vidēns autem diabolus eam [189] dē verbīs dominī dubitāre, inquit: "Nēquāquam moriēminī, sed eritis sīcut diī,

alloquor, alloquī, allocūtus sum: to speak to; address
antīquus, -a, -um: old, ancient
audeō, audēre, ausus sum: to dare
comedō, -ere, comēdī, comestum: to eat
cōram (+ abl.): in the presence of
cūr: why
diabolus, -ī m.: the devil
dubitō (1): to doubt; hesitate (over)
fēmina, -ae f.: woman
forte: by chance (adv.)
interrogātiō, -ōnis f.: interrogation

lignum, -ī n.: wood; tree
morior, morī, mortuus sum: to die
nēquāquam: no way; by no means
paradīsus, -ī m.: paradise
persuāsiō, -ōnis f.: persuasion
praecipiō, -ere, praecēpī, praeceptum (+ dat.): to instruct, command
prōrumpō, -ere, prōrūpī, prōruptum: to rush forward
sententia, -ae f.: opinion; sentence
sīcut: just like
superō (1): to overcome

(In) *Sententiārum* II.° (librō): *(In) the second (book) of Sentences;* Nogarola here paraphrases from the *Sentences,* a 12th-century work of theology by Peter Lombard; these remarks are from 2.21.3 (*PL* 192.695)
hostis antīquus: *the ancient enemy;* that is, the devil
nōn est ausus: *did not dare;* the verb is semi-deponent and sets up *prōrumpere*
sub interrogātiōne: *under (the pretense of) questioning;* that is, the devil did not set out in a straight-forward way to persuade her, but rather began by asking questions
"Cūr praecēpit...bonum et malum": the dialogue within Peter Lombard's statement paraphrases Genesis 3.1–5
nē comederētis: *that you not eat;* an imperfect subjunctive in an indirect command set up by *praecēpit*
Nē...moriāmur: *So that we don't die;* negative purpose clause
diī: *gods;* nom./pl./masc., an alternate form of *deī*

scientēs bonum et malum."

2.2 Vel etiam propter maiōrem praeceptī contemptum, nam Genesis II.° vidētur dominus Ādae nōn Ēvae praecēpisse, cum dīcit: "Tulit ergō dominus Deus hominem et posuit eum in paradīsō voluptātis ut operārētur et cūstōdīret illum" (et nōn dīxit "ut operārentur et custōdīrent illum")— "et praecēpit eī" (et nōn "eīs")— "ex omnī lignō comede" (et nōn "comedite")—

---

capitulum, -ī n.: chapter

comedō, -ere, comēdī, comestum: to eat

contemptus, -ūs m.: contempt

custōdiō, -īre, custōdīvī, custōdītum: to guard

Genesis, -is f.: the Book of Genesis

lignum, -ī n.: wood; tree

maior, maius: greater (comp. adj.)

operor, operārī, operātus sum: to work (in), be occupied (with)

paradīsus, -ī m.: paradise

praeceptum, -ī n.: a command

praecipiō, -ere, praecēpī, praeceptum (+ dat.): to command

propter (+ acc.): on account of

voluptās, -tātis f.: pleasure

---

scientēs bonum et malum: *knowing good and evil;* the words *bonum* and *malum* here are neuter substantive adjectives acting as abstract nouns

Vel etiam (magis peccāvit Ādam): *Or even (more greatly did Adam sin);* this idea, or a similar one, seems to be implicit

maiōrem praeceptī contemptum: *the greater contempt for (God's) command;* objective genitive; Nogarola explains that God explicitly forbid Adam, not Eve, from eating the fruit

(in) Genesis II.° (capitulō): *(in) the second (chapter) of Genesis;* Gen. 2:15–17

ut operārētur et cūstōdīret illum: *to work in and guard it;* purpose clause

et nōn dīxit: *and (God) did not say;* these words are Nogarola breaking into the quotation, as she does again with *et nōn* three times later in the sentence; each time she emphasizes that the form is singular, meaning that God was commanding only Adam, not Adam and Eve

"in quōcumque enim diē comedēris, morte moriēris" (et nōn "moriēminī"). Et hoc quia magis aestimābat hominem quam mulierem.

2.3 Nec vidētur id fēcisse mulierem quia Deī similem sē fierī magis crēdiderit, sed propter fragilitātem potius et voluptātem; unde "Vīdit mulier quod bonum esset lignum ad vēscendum et

---

aestimō (1): to value
comedō, -ere, comēdī, comestum: to eat
fragilitās, -tātis f.: frailty
lignum, -ī n.: wood; tree
morior, morī, mortuus sum: to die
potius: rather
propter (+ acc.): on account of

quīcumque, quaecumque, quodcumque: whoever, whatever
similis, -e (+ gen. or dat.): like, similar to
unde: from where; from which thing; that's why
vēscor, vēscī, -: to eat
voluptās, -tātis f.: pleasure; the desire for pleasure

---

morte moriēris: *you will die in death*
Et hoc (est) quia: *And this (is) because*
aestimābat: *he valued;* the subject is still God
quam mulierem: *than the woman;* the *quam* is comparative, set up by *magis*
Nec vidētur id fēcisse mulierem: *Nor does it seem that the woman did this;* in Classical Latin the verb *vidētur* would take a nom. subject (*mulier*), but here it is used impersonally to set up an acc. and inf.; Nogarola is here countering Foscarini's contention that Eve wanted to be like God, an unforgivable sin (1.1)
unde "Vīdit mulier…": *that's why (it is written) "The woman saw…";* Nogarola leaves implicit a verb like *scrībitur;* the quotation is Gen. 3:6
quod bonum esset lignum: *that the tree was good;* post-classical Latin frequently uses a quod-clause rather than acc. and inf. for indirect statement
bonum…ad vescendum: *good to eat;* literally "good for eating"; *ad* + gerund to express purpose

37

pulchrum oculīs aspectūque dēlectābile, et tulit dē frūctū illīus et comēdit deditque virō suō" (et nōn dīxit "ut esset similis Deō").

2.4 Et nisi Ādam [190] comēdisset, peccātum ultrā prōgressum nōn fuisset. Unde nōn dīcitur "Sī Ēva nōn peccāsset, Chrīstus nōn fuisset incarnātus," sed "Sī Ādam nōn peccāsset." Unde mulier, quamvīs cum eō, dē quō erat trānsducta,

---

aspectus, -ūs m.: appearance
Chrīstus, -ī m.: Christ
comedō, -ere, comēdī, comēsum: to eat
dēlectābilis, -e: delightful
frūctus, -ūs m.: fruit
incarnō (1): to make incarnate, make into flesh
prōgredior, -gredī, -gressus sum: to go forward, proceed

quamvīs (+ subj.): although
similis, -e (+ gen. or dat.): like, similar to
trānsdūcō, -ere, trānsdūxī, trānsductum: to bring over; transfer; take
ultrā: beyond, further (adv.)
unde: from where; from which thing; that's why

---

tulit dē frūctū illīus: *took of its fruit;* in post-classical Latin, *dē* + abl. takes on a partitive sense
virō suō: *to her husband;* that is, to Adam
et nōn dīxit: *and it did not say;* this again is Nogarola breaking into the quotation to emphasize her point
ut esset similis: *in order that she be similar;* purpose clause
peccātum...prōgressum nōn fuisset: *the sin would not have proceeded;* the verb is a pluperfect subjunctive (= CL *prōgressum esset*), and the sentence is a past contrary-to-fact condition
nōn dīcitur: *it is not said;* the following quotation is a twist on a common saying ("If Adam had not sinned, Christ would not have been made flesh")
peccāsset: = *peccāvisset*, the syncopated form of the pluperfect subjunctive
quamvīs cum eō...morārētur: *although she (Eve) stayed...with him (Adam);* that is, they were both in the Garden of Eden; the language echoes Boccaccio's Life of Eve (*Dē Mulieribus Clārīs* 1.5)
dē quō erat trānsducta: *from whom she had been taken;* a reference to Eve being created from Adam's rib in Gen. 2:21–22

in paradīsī dēliciīs morārētur, prīmō tamen malae suāsiōnis īnsultum perpessa est, nihil vērō, nisi sē ipsam, generis posteritātem laesisset priōris creātī hominis assēnsū nōn praestitō. Igitur nōn Ēva posteritātī, sed sibi perīculō fuit. Homō autem Ādam sibi et cūnctae propāgātiōnī sequentī trānsdūcere maculam propīnāvit.

---

assēnsus, -ūs m.: assent

creō (1): to create

cunctus, -a, -um: all

dēliciae, -ārum f.: delights, pleasures

igitur: therefore

īnsultus, -ī m.: assault, attack

laedō, -ere, laesī, laesum: to hurt

macula, -ae f.: stain

moror, morārī, morātus sum: to delay; stay

paradīsus, -ī m.: paradise

perīculum, -ī n.: danger

perpetior, perpetī, perpessus sum: to endure to the full

posteritās, -tātis f.: future time; posterity

praestō, praestāre, praestitī, praestitum: to offer, give

prīmō: first (adv.)

prior, prius: prior, first

prōpāgātiō, -ōnis f.: propagation, offspring

propīnō (1): to supply, pass on

trānsdūcō, -ere, trānsdūxī, trānsductum: to bring over, transfer

vērō: but; and (postpositive)

---

perpessa est: *she endured;* the subject is Eve and the object *īnsultum*

nihil...laesisset: *in no way...would she have harmed;* the *nihil* is functioning adverbially; *laesisset* is a pluperfect subjunctive as the then-clause of a past contrary-to-fact condition whose if-clause is the following ablative absolute

priōris creātī hominis: *of the first created human;* Adam

assēnsū nōn praestitō: *if the consent were not given;* ablative absolute with a conditional sense

nōn Ēva posteritātī, sed sibi perīculō fuit: *Eve was not a danger to posterity, but to herself;* double dative construction: the *perīculō* is a dative of purpose, while *posteritātī* and *sibi* are datives of reference

trānsdūcere maculam propīnāvit: *passed on a stain that transfers (itself)*

Proinde Ādam hominum generandōrum auctor existēns et perditiōnis prīmus fuit occāsiō; quamobrem prius in virō, deinde in fēminā generis hūmānī est celebrāta cūrātiō, cum (post expulsiōnem immundī spīritūs ā virō) dē sinagōgā surgēns persānandō accessit ad fēminam.

2.5 Quod autem ā iūstō iūdice dūriōrī poenā damnāta fuerit, [191] hoc perspicuē vidētur in contrārium,

accēdō, -ere, accessī, accessum: to approach, go to

auctor, -ōris m.: source, ancestor

celebrō (1): to celebrate

contrārius, -a, -um: contrary

cūrātiō, -ōnis f.: cure; healing

damnō (1): to condemn

existō, -ere, existitī, existitum: to come forward; arise

expulsiō, -ōnis f.: expulsion

fēmina, -ae f.: woman

generō (1): to generate, produce

hūmānus, -a, -um: human

immundus, -a, -um: unclean, impure

iūdex, iūdicis m.: judge

iūstus, -a, -um: just, fair

occāsiō, -ōnis f.: occasion; cause

perditiō, -ōnis f.: ruin

persānō (1): to heal completely

perspicuē: clearly

prius: first (adv.)

proinde: from there, so then

quamobrem: that's why, for this reason

sinagōga, -ae f.: synagogue

spīritus, -ūs m.: spirit

surgō, -ere, surrēxī, surrēctum: to rise

prius in virō, deinde in fēminā: *first in (the case of) a man, then a woman;* Nogarola is referring Mark 1:21–31 (= Luke 4:32–39) where Jesus heals a man possessed by an unclean spirit in a synagogue, and then cures Simon's mother-in-law of a fever

expulsiōnem immundī spīritūs ā virō: *the expulsion of the unclean spirit from a man;* note that *spīritūs* is genitive agreeing with *immundī* and the prepositional phrase *ā virō* is abl. of separation, not agent

persānandō accessit ad fēminam: *he came to a woman to heal (her);* the *persānandō* is a gerund acting as a dat. of purpose

Quod...damnāta fuerit: *As to the fact that she was condemned;* a noun clause with a subjunctive of reported reason, referring back to Foscarini's words in 1.1

in contrārium: *to the contrary; in* + accusative is used to convey a sense of motion

nam dīxit Deus mulierī: "Multiplicābō aerumnās tuās et conceptūs tuōs; in dolōre pariēs fīliōs et sub virī potestāte eris." Ādae vērō dīxit: "Quia audīstī vōcem uxōris tuae et comēdistī dē lignō, ex quō praecēperam tibi nē comederēs" (ecce quod vidētur quod Deus sōlum praecēpit Ādae, et nōn Ēvae) "maledicta terra in opere tuō,

---

aerumna, -ae f.: hardship

comedō, -ere, comēdī, comēsum: to eat

conceptus, -ūs m.: childbirth

ecce: look!

fīlius, -ī m.: son; (pl.) children

lignum, -ī n.: wood; tree

maledictus, -a, -um: cursed

multiplicō (1): to multiply

opus, operis n.: work

pariō, -ere, peperī, partum: to give birth to

potestās, -tātis f.: power

praecipiō, -ere, praecēpī, praeceptum (+ dat.): to command

sōlum: alone (adv.)

uxor, uxōris f.: wife

vērō: and, but (postpositive)

"Multiplicābō...eris": *"I will multiply...you will be"*; Genesis 3:16

aerumnās...tuōs: *the pains of childbirth;* literally "the pains and childbirths"; the expression of one idea through two is the rhetorical device hendiadys

"Quia...revertēris": *"Because...you will return"*; Genesis 3:17–19

audīstī: *you have listened;* syncopated form of *audīvistī*

dē lignō: *from the tree;* referring to the Tree of Knowledge in the Garden of Eden

nē comederēs: *that you not eat;* negative indirect command set up by *praecēperam*

ecce quod vidētur quod: *look at the fact that it seems that;* Nogarola here interjects to note that God only commanded Adam, not Eve; the first *quod* is starting a noun clause, while the second starts an indirect statement with *vidētur*

sōlum: *only;* acting as an adverb modifying *praecēpit*

maledicta (erit) terra: *cursed (will be) the ground*

in labōribus comedēs ex eā cūnctīs diēbus vītae tuae. Spīnās et tribulōs germinābit tibi et comedēs herbās terrae. In sūdōre vultūs tuī vēscēris pāne tuō, dōnec revertāris in terram, dē quā assūmptus es, quia pulvis es et in pulverem revertēris." Ecce quod dūrior vidētur poena Ādae quam Ēvae, nam eī dīxit "in pulverem revertēris" et nōn Ēvae, et "ultimum terribilium est mors":

assūmō, -ere, assūmpsī, assumptum: to take	pulvis, pulveris m.: dust
comedō, -ere, comēdī, comēsum: to eat	revertor, revertī, reversus sum: to return
cūnctus, -a, -um: all	spīna, -ae f.: thorn-bush
dōnec (+ subj.): until	sūdor, -ōris m.: sweat
ecce: look!	terribilis, -e: terrible
germinō (1): to grow, cause to grow	tribulus, -ī m.: spiny plant
herba, -ae f.: grass, plants, weeds	ultimus, -a, -um: ultimate
pānis, -is m.: bread	vēscor, vēscī (+abl.): to feed on

ex eā: *from it;* referring back to *terra*

cūnctīs diēbus: *all the days;* abl. of extent of time, a common post-classical construction

In sūdōre vultūs tuī: *by the sweat of your brow;* the *vultūs tuī* is gen./sg./masc.

dē quā assūmptus es: *from which you were taken;* referring back to the creation of humans from mud in Genesis 2:7

Ecce quod: *Look at the fact that;* the *quod* here introduces a noun clause

nam eī dīxit: *for he said to him;* *eī* is referring to Adam, while the subject of *dīxit* is God

"ultimum terribilium est mors": *death is the ultimate of terrible things;* rather than agreeing with the feminine subject (*mors*), the gender of *ultimum* is neuter as a substantive: "the ultimate (thing) of terrible (ones)"; the idea is from Aristotle (*Nic. Ethics* 3.6.6, 1115a) and is commonly repeated by scholastic authors, usually with death as the *finis* ("end") of all terrible things

ergō vidētur maiōrem fuisse poenam Ādae quam Ēvae.

2.6 Haec ut tuae voluntātī mōrem gererem scrīpsī, sed cum timōre tamen, quia nōn hoc opus fēmineum est; sed [192] tū prō tuā hūmānitāte, sī quid ineptē scrīptum inveniēs, ēmendābis.

3.1 Rēspōnsiō Lodovīcī: Subtīlissimē Ēvae causam dēfendis et ita dēfendis, ut, sī vir nātus nōn fuissem, mē tuārum partium tūtōrem cōnstituissēs.

---

cōnstituō, -ere, cōnstituī, cōnstitūtum: to make, set-up
dēfendō, -ere, dēfendī, dēfensum: to defend
ēmendō (1): to correct
fēmineus, -a, -um: womanly
hūmānitas, -tātis f.: kindness, humanity
ineptus, -a, -um: inept
inveniō, -īre, invēnī, inventum: to discover

Lodovīcus, -ī m.: Ludovico (Foscarini)
nāscor, nāscī, nātus sum: to be born
opus, operis n.: work
rēspōnsiō, -onis f.: response
scrībō, -ere, scrīpsī, scrīptum: to write
subtīlis, -e: subtle, exquisite, exact
timor, -ōris m.: fear
tūtor, -ōris m.: defender
voluntās, -tātis f.: desire

Haec...scrīpsī: *I have written...these things;* referring to her arguments
voluntātī mōrem gererem: *in order to indulge your desire;* literally "bear the manner"; purpose clause
nōn...opus fēmineum: *not...womanly work;* the words seem aimed to deflect criticism, but they are deeply ironic, given that Nogarola's overall argument is that it is not wrong or inappropriate for women to seek knowledge
sī (ali)quid ineptē scrīptum inveniēs: *if you discover anything ineptly written;* the if-clause of a future more vivid condition; the *ali-* drops out before *sī, nisi, num,* and *ne*
sī vir nātus nōn fuissem: *if I not been born a man;* pluperfect subjunctive (= CL *nātus nōn essem*), the if-clause of a past contrafactual condition embedded within a result clause (*ut...cōnstituissēs*)
tuārum partium: *of your faction;* the word *pars* with a sense of "party" or "faction" can be plural in form but singular in meaning

Sed vēritātī, quae firmissimīs est fīxa rādīcibus, haerēns tua castra tuīs iaculīs oppugnāre īnstituī, et fundāmenta, quae sacrārum līterārum testimōniō negārī possent, nē contrādīcendī māteria dēsit, nunc impugnābō.

3.2 Ēva ignōrāns incōnstānsque peccāvit, ex quō tibi levius peccāsse vidētur.

---

contrādīcō, -ere, contrādīxī, contrādictum: to contradict

dēsum, dēesse, dēfuī, dēfutūrum: to be lacking

firmus, -a, -um: firm

fīxus, -a, -um: fixed

fundāmentum, -ī n.: foundation

haereō, -ēre, haesī, haesum: to adhere, cling

iaculum, -ī n.: javelin; weapon

ignōrāns, -ntis: ignorant

ignōrō (1): to disregard

impugnō (1): to attack

incōnstāns, -ntis: inconsistent

īnstituō, -ere, īnstituī, īnstitūtum: to set up, decide

levius: more lightly (comp. adv.)

lītera, -ae f.: letter; writings (pl.)

māteria, -ae f.: material

negō (1): to deny

oppugnō (1): to attack

rādīx, rādīcis f.: root

sacer, -cra, -crum: holy

testimōnium, -ī n.: evidence

vēritas, -tātis f.: truth

---

vēritātī…(ego) haerēns: *(I), clinging to the truth;* the *haerēns* agrees with the implicit first-person subject of *īnstituī* ("I decided"); the phrase *vēritātī…haerēns* echoes Augustine *Dē Dīversīs Quaestiōnibus* 51.4 (*PL* 40.33)

firmissimīs est fīxa rādīcibus: *has been fixed by the firmest roots;* a paraphrase of Cicero's description of virtue (*Phil.* 4.5.13)

tua castra tuīs iaculīs oppugnāre: *to attack your camp with your own weapons;* that is, he will use the evidence she has cited to argue against her position

fundāmenta: *the foundations (of your argument);* direct object of *impugnābō*

quae…negārī possent: *which can be denied on the basis of the testimony of the sacred literature;* Foscarini claims that sacred literature will undermine the foundations of Nogarola's argument

ex quō…vidētur: *from which thing she seems;* the *quō* refers to the whole previous clause; *levius* here is a comp. adv.; *peccāsse* is a syncopated version of *peccāvisse*

Ignōrantia eōrum praesertim quae scīre dēbēmus nōs nōn excūsat, quia scrīptum est: "Sī quis ignōrat, ignōrābitur"; "Oculōs quōs culpa claudit, poena aperit"; "Quī stultus est in culpā, sapiēns erit in poenā," praesertim cum error peccantis negligentiā occurrit. Ignōrantia enim mulieris, nāta ex arrogantiā, nōn excūsat. Velutī Aristotīlēs et iūriscōnsultī, [193] quī vēram profitentur philosophiam,

aperiō, -īre, aperuī, apertum: to open	**negligentia, -ae f.**: negligence
Aristotīlēs, -is m.: Aristotle	**occurrō, -ere, occurrī, occursum**: to
arrogantia, -ae f.: arrogance	occur, happen
claudō, -ere, clausī, clausum: to shut	**philosophia, -ae f.**: philosophy
culpa, -ae f.: guilt	**praesertim**: especially (adv.)
error, -ōris m.: error	**profiteor, profitērī, professus sum**: to
excūsō (1): to excuse	profess
ignōrāns, -ntis: ignorant (of)	**sapiēns, -ntis**: wise
ignōrantia, -ae f.: ignorance	**scrībō, -ere, scrīpsī, scrīptum**: to write
ignōrō (1): to disregard	**stultus, -ī m.**: a fool
iūriscōnsultus, -ī m.: legal expert	**velutī**: just as
nāscor, nāscī, nātus sum: to be born	**vērus, -a, -um**: true

"Sī quis ignōrat, ignōrābitur": *"If anyone ignores (this), he himself will be ignored";* the quotation is 1 Corinthians 14:38; Paul is referring to his prescription that women remain submissive and silent in church (1 Corinth. 14:34–36)

"Oculōs...aperit": *"The eyes which guilt closes, punishment opens";* a quotation from Gregory the Great, *Moralia* 15.51 (*PL* 75: 1111)

"Quī stultus est...in poenā": *He who is a fool...in punishment;* this quotation is from Gratian's *Dēcrētum* (Distinction 38, chapter 10)

cum...neglegentiā occurrit: *when the error...occurs through negligence;* abl. of means

Aristotīlēs: Aristotle's *Nicomachean Ethics* 3.5.8 (1113b); as found in Thomas Aquinas's *Summa Theologica* (IIb q.150 a.4)

et iūricōnsultī, quī vēram profitentur philosophiam: *Aristotle and the legal experts who profess the true philosophy;* that is, Christian legal experts; the idea is found in Aquinas (see above note), but it might have been repeated in legal texts

duplicī poenā ēbriōs et ignōrantēs dignōs iūdicant. Nesciō etiam, quōnam pactō tū, quae per tot annōrum cursūs ab Ēvā distās, ipsīus sēnsum damnās, cuius scientiam in paradīsō summō omnium rērum opifice dīvīnitus creātam serpentem astūtissimum praesentem timuisse scrībis, quia nōn fuit ausus in verba persuāsiōnis prōrumpere, sed sub interrogātiōne eam allocūtus est.

alloquor, alloquī, allocūtus sum: to address, speak to

astūtus, -a, -um: cunning

audeō, audēre, ausus sum: to dare

creō (1): create

cursus, -ūs m.: course, passage

damnō (1): to condemn

dignus, -a, -um (+ abl.): deserving

distō (1): be distant

dīvīnitus: divinely (adv.)

duplex, -is: twofold

ēbrius, -a, -um: drunk

ignōrāns, -ntis: ignorant (of)

ignōrō (1): to disregard

interrogātiō, -ōnis f.: questioning

iūdicō (1): to judge

-nam: marks an emphatic question

nesciō, -īre, nescīvī, nescītum: to not know, not understand

opifex, opificis m.: craftsman

pactum, -ī n.: agreement

paradīsus, -ī m: paradise, Eden

persuādeō, -ēre, persuāsī, persuāsum: to persuade

praesēns, -ntis: present; powerful

prōrumpō, -ere, prōrūpī, prōruptum: to rush forth

scientia, -ae f.: knowledge

scrībō, -ere, scrīpsī, scrīptum: to write

sēnsus, -ūs m.: sense, mental capacity

serpēns, serpentis m.: snake

summus, -a, -um: highest

tot: so many

quōnam pactō: *how on earth; quō* is the interrogative adj. with the enclitic particle *-nam* emphasizing the question, and *pactō* is from *pactum* ("agreement"); literally, *quō pactō* is "by what agreement" but it is a common idiom for "how"

quae...distās: *(you) who...are distant;* Nogarola is subject of *distās* and *damnās*

per tot annōrum cursūs: *through the passage of so many years;* that is, Nogarola is distant in time from Eve by so many years

cuius scientiam...scrībis: *whose knowledge, divinely created in paradise by the highest craftsman, you write that the most cunning, powerful serpent feared;* the verb *scrībis* sets up an indirect statement, in which *serpentem* is the subject, *timuisse* the verb, and *scientiam* the object

3.3 Dē incōnstantiā vērō prōcēdentēs operātiōnēs vituperābiliōrēs sunt. Quemadmodum enim operātiōnēs sequentēs habitum cōnstantissimum et firmātum sunt laude digniōrēs et speciē differunt ā praecēdentibus, ita ex incōnstantiā prōcēdentēs operātiōnēs maiōrī cēnsūrā pūniendae, quia incōnstantia, per sē mala, addita peccātō malō facit ipsum dēterius.

addō, -ere, addidī, additum: to add to
cēnsūra, -ae f.: blame
cōnstāns, -ntis: constant
dēterior, dēterius: worse (comp. adj.)
differō, differre, distulī, dīlātum: to differ
dignus, -a, -um (+ abl.): worthy
firmō (1): to strengthen
habitus, -ūs m.: behavior
incōnstāns, -ntis: inconsistent
incōnstantia, -ae f.: inconsistency
laus, laudis f.: praise

maior, maius: greater (comp. adj.)
operātio, -ōnis f.: action
praecēdō, -ere, praecessī, praecessum: to precede
prōcēdō, -ere, prōcessī, prōcessum: to proceed
pūniō, -īre, pūnīvī, pūnītum: to punish
quemadmodum: to the extent that
speciēs, -ēī f.: type, species
vērō: and, but (postpositive)
vituperābilis, -e: blameworthy

habitum...firmātum: *constant and firm behavior;* direct object of *sequentēs*
speciē: *by type;* ablative of respect
ā praecēdentibus: *from the ones just mentioned;* literally, "from the preceding ones," that is, the acts proceeding from inconsistency
maiōrī cēnsūrā: *greater blame;* abl./sg./fem.; the form of the comparative is equivalent to CL *maiōre*
pūniendae (sunt): *must be punished;* passive periphrastic; the subject is *operātiōnēs*
mala, addita: both agree with the nom. *incōnstantia*
facit ipsum dēterius: *makes it worse;* a double accusative; Foscarini argues that since inconstancy is bad in and of itself, it does not excuse a sin but rather adds to it and makes it worse

3.4 Custōdia etiam Ādae commissa sociam nōn excūsat, quia fūrēs, quōrum operā paterfamiliās cōnfīdēns [194] ūtitur, ultimō suppliciō nōn pūniuntur, velutī extrāneī et illī, dē quibus nūlla est habita cōnfīdentia.

3.5 Fragilitās etiam mulieris nōn fuit peccātī causa, velutī scrībis, sed superbia, quoniam prōmissiō daemonis fuit scientiae, quae arrogantēs efficit et secundum Apostolum īnflat.

apostolus, -ī m.: apostle
arrogāns, -ntis: arrogant
committō, -ere, commīsī,
commissum: to entrust
cōnfīdēns, -ntis: confident
cōnfīdentia, -ae f.: confidence
custōdia, -ae f.: guard
daemōn, -onis m.: demon
efficiō, -ere, effēcī, effectum: to make
excūsō (1): to excuse
extrāneus, -a, -um: outsider
familia, -ae f.: family; household
fragilitās, -tātis f.: frailty
fūr, fūris m.: thief

īnflō (1): to inflate; puff up (with pride)
opera, -ae f.: work, labor
prōmissiō, -ōnis f.: promise
pūniō, -īre, -īvī, -ītum: to punish
quoniam: because, since
scientia, -ae f.: knowledge
scrībō, -ere, scrīpsī, scrīptum: to write
secundum (+ acc.): according to
socia, -ae f.: partner
superbia, -ae f.: pride
supplicium, -ī n.: punishment
ūtor, ūtī, ūsus sum (+abl.): to use
velutī: just as, as

Custōdia…Ādae commissa: *the guardianship entrusted to Adam;* Foscarini here rebuts an argument that seems to have been removed from the text (Introduction IX)

quia fūrēs…habita cōnfīdentia: *because thieves, whose labor the head of the household uses with trust, are not punished with the utmost punishment, unlike outsiders and those in whom no confidence has been placed;* just as family members are treated more leniently than strangers, Eve should be treated more leniently as well

paterfamiliās: *the head of the household;* a technical term that combines *pater* and *familiās,* which is the archaic genitive of *familia*

quae (hominēs) arrogantēs efficit: *which makes (people) arrogant;* a double accusative, with the first noun implicit

Apostolum: *the Apostle;* that is, Paul; the quotation is from 1 Corinthians 8:1

"Initium" enim apud Ecclēsiasticum "superbia fuit omnis peccātī." Et licet aliae cōnsecūtae sint, illa tamen prīncipālior, quoniam carō oboediēns erat hominī in statū innocentiae existentī et nōn contrāria ratiōnī. Fuit ergō prīmus mōtus inōrdinātus appetītus appetendī quod nātūrae suae nōn competēbat, velutī Augustīnus Orōsiō scrīpsit:

appetītus, -ūs m.: appetite, desire
appetō, -ere, -īvī, -ītum: to seek, desire
Augustīnus, -ī m.: Augustine
carō, carnis f.: flesh
competō, -ere, competīvī, competītum: to be suitable
cōnsequor, cōnsequī, cōnsecūtus sum: to follow, come after
contrārius, -a, -um: contrary
existō, -ere, existitī, existitum: to appear, exist
initium, -ī n.: beginning
innocentia, -ae f.: innocence

inōrdinātus, -a, -um: inordinate; excessive
licet (+ subj.): although
mōtus, -ūs m.: movement, impulse
oboediēns, -ientis: obedient
Orōsius, -ī m.: Orosius (name)
prīncipālis, -e: first, chief, principal
quoniam: because, since
ratiō, -ōnis f.: reason
scrībō, -ere, scrīpsī, scrīptum: to write
status, -ūs m.: state
superbia, -ae f.: arrogance
velutī: just as

Ecclēsiasticum: the quotation is Sirach 10:13; the Hebrew Book of Sirach is called Ecclesiasticus in the Latin Vulgate

aliae (causae) cōnsecūtae sint: *other (causes of sin) have followed;* aliae is acting substantively

illa (causa) tamen prīncipālior (fuit): *that (cause) however (was) the first;* the *prīncipālior* is a comparative giving the sense of "first" both in time and in importance, so arrogance was the principal cause of sin, though other causes followed

Fuit ergō prīmus mōtus: *Therefore the first impulse (to sin)*

appetītus appetendī (id) quod: *appetite for seeking that which;* appetendī is an objective genitive, which has as its own object an implicit *id*

Orōsiō: *Orosius;* Orosius was a student of Augustine; the general idea seems to be in *PL* 42.671 (cf. *PL* 32.1308), though Foscarini's formulation of the idea comes from Thomas Aquinas's *Summa Theologica* (IIb q.163 a.1)

"Homō, ēlātus superbiā, suāsiōnī serpentis oboediēns, praecepta Deī contempsit"; dīxit enim adversārius Ēvae: "Aperientur oculī vestrī et eritis sīcut diī, scientēs bonum et malum." Nec crēdidisset mulier, ut ait Augustīnus super Genesī, suāsiōnī daemonis, [195] nisi propriae potestātis amor ipsam invāsisset, quī rīvus ex superbiae fonte prōcēdit. Nē ab Augustīnō discēdam,

adversārius, -ī m.: adversary

aiō, -, -: to say (defective)

aperiō, -īre, aperuī, apertum: to open

Augustīnus, -ī m.: Augustine

contemnō, -ere, contempsī, contemptum: to disregard

daemōn, -onis m.: demon, devil

discēdō, -ere, discessī, discessum: to depart from

ēlātus, -a, -um: raised, exalted

fōns, -ntis m.: font, fountain

Genesis, -is f.: the Book of Genesis

invādō, -ere, invāsī, invāsum: to invade

oboediō, -īre, oboedīvī, oboedītum (+ dat.): to obey

potestās, -tātis f.: power

praeceptum, -ī n.: a command

prōcēdo, -ere, prōcessī, prōcessum: to proceed

proprius, -a, -um: own

rīvus, -ī m.: stream

serpēns, -ntis m.: snake

sīcut: like

suāsiō, -ōnis f.: persuasion

super (+ abl.): over (space); concerning

superbia, -ae f.: arrogance

vester, -tra, -trum: your (pl.)

adversārius: *the adversary;* that is, the serpent

"Aperientur...bonum et malum": Genesis 3:5

eritis sīcut diī: *you will be like gods; diī* is an alternate form for *deī*

scientēs bonum et malum: *knowing good and evil; bonum* and *malum* are substantives acting as abstract nouns

Nec crēdidisset mulier...suāsiōnī daemonis: *The woman would not have believed...the persuasion of the demon;* the verb *crēdere* takes a dative object (*suāsiōnī*); pluperfect subjunctive as the then-clause of a past contrafactual condition

Augustīnus super Genesī: *Augustine concerning Genesis;* the statement is from *Dē Genesī ad Litteram* (*PL* 34.445)

quī rīvus ex superbiae fonte prōcēdit: *which stream (of love of her own power) flows from the font of pride;* a reference to the *propriae potestātis amor* from the previous line

dum voluit Ēva rapere dīvīnitātem, perdidit fēlīcitātem.

3.6 Et verba illa ("Sī Ādam nōn peccāsset etc.") mē in sententiā cōnfirmant; quia ita fortasse peccāvit Ēva quod, velutī daemonēs nōn meruērunt redēmptiōnem, ita fortasse Ēva! Iocī tantum causā loquor, sed fēlīx fuit Ādae culpa, quae tālem meruit habēre redēmptōrem.

cōnfirmō (1): to strengthen; confirm	**loquor, loquī, locūtus sum**: to speak
culpa, -ae f.: fault, failure	**mereō, -ēre, meruī, meritum**: to merit
daemōn, -onis m.: demon	**perdō, -ere, perdidī, perditum**: to lose
dīvīnitās, -tātis f.: divinity	**rapiō, -ere, rapuī, raptum**: to seize
fēlīcitās, -tātis f.: happiness	**redēmptiō, -ōnis f.**: redemption
fēlīx, fēlīcis: happy; fortunate	**redēmptor, -ōris m.**: redeemer
fortasse: perhaps	**sententia, -ae f.**: opinion
iocus, -ī m.: joke	**velutī**: just as

dum voluit Ēva: *when Eve wished...; dum* can mean "when" in post-classical Latin; the statement is from Augustine *Ēnārrātiōnēs in Psalmōs* 68.1.9 (*PL* 36.848), yet Augustine had used plural verbs, referring to Adam, Eve, and the devil

Et verba illa ("Sī Ādam nōn peccāsset etc."): *And those words ("If Adam had not sinned etc.");* this is a reference to the common saying "if Adam had not sinned, Christ would not have been made incarnate..."; Nogarola used this saying in 2.4 to suggest that Adam's sin had more effect on later generations

quod...fortasse Ēva: *that...perhaps Eve (did not merit redemption);* Foscarini here uses *quod* rather than *ut* for his result clause, which implicitly reuses the verb "to merit" from its subordinate clause; he had mentioned in 1.1 that Eve's sin might be unforgivable

Iocī tantum causā loquor: *I am only joking; tantum* is the adverb rather than the adjective; *causā* + gen. is an idiom that means "for the sake of"

quae tālem meruit habēre redēmptōrem: *which merited to have such a redeemer;* that is, Jesus; Foscarini is referencing the belief that Jesus came to Earth to redeem the world from the sinful state that Adam caused

3.7 Et nē tandem ā scrīptīs tuīs discēdam, omnēs poenās virī patitur mulier, et quia multiplicātae sunt eius aerumnae, nōn sōlum moritur, vēscitur sūdōris poenā, prohibētur per Cherubim et flammeōs gladiōs accessū paradīsī, sed ultrā omnia quae commūnia sunt, sōla cum dolōre parit et virō subdita est.

3.8 Sed quia in tantā rē nōn est satis tua cōnfūtāsse, nisi etiam nostra cōnfirmēmus,

---

accessus, -ūs m.: entry; entrance

aerumna, -ae f.: hardship

Cherubim: Cherubim, a kind of angel (undeclined)

commūnis, -e: common

cōnfirmō (1): to strengthen; develop

cōnfūtō (1): to diminish; refute

discēdō, -ere, discessī, discessum: to depart

flammeus, -a, -um: flaming, fiery

gladius, -ī m.: sword

morior, morī, mortuus sum: to die

multiplicō (1): to multiply, increase

paradīsus, -ī m.: paradise

pariō, -ere, peperī, partum: to give birth

prohibeō, -ēre, -uī, -itum: to forbid

satis: enough

scrībō, -ere, scrīpsī, scrīptum: to write

subdō, -ere, subdidī, subditum: to place under; subject to

sūdor, -ōris m.: sweat; hard labor

tandem: at last

ultrā (+ acc.): beyond, more than

vēscor, vēscī, -: to eat

ā scrīptīs tuīs : *from what you have written;* Foscarini is referring back to Nogarola's argument in 2.5 that Adam's penalty was greater than Eve's

nōn sōlum moritur, vēscitur sūdōris poenā, prohibētur...accessū paradīsī: *she not only dies, she eats by penalty of hard labor, she is forbidden...entry to paradise;* these punishments are shared by both Adam and Eve in Gen. 3:17–24

nōn sōlum moritur: *not only does she die; sōlum* here is the adverb "only"

vēscitur sūdōris poenā: *she eats by penalty of hard labor; poenā* is abl. of means

sed ultrā...sunt: *but beyond all punishments which are common (to both);* these additional punishments are from Gen. 3:16

tua cōnfūtāsse...nostra cōnfirmēmus: *to have refuted your (arguments)...confirm my own (arguments);* the *tua* and *nostra* are acting substantively; *cōnfūtāsse = cōnfūtāvisse;* Foscarini uses the first person plural to refer to himself, as is common in Latin

crēdidit Ēva Deō similis fierī et invidēns optāvit quod Spīritum [196] Sānctum laedit.

3.9 Omnis etiam Ādae culpa Ēvae ascrībitur, quia Aristotīle teste quidquid est causa causae est causa causātī; immō omnis prīma causa plūs īnfluit in effectum quam secunda. Prīncipium enim eōdem Aristotīle teste in quōcumque genere maximum dīcitur; immō plūs quam dīmidium tōtīus habētur.

Aristotīlēs, -is m.: Aristotle

ascrībō, -ere, ascrīpsī, ascrīptum: to ascribe; assign

causō (1): to cause

culpa, -ae f.: fault

dīmidium, -ī n.: half

effectus, -ūs m.: effect, result

genus, generis n.: kind; genus

immō: indeed

īnfluō, -ere, īnflūxī, īnflūxum: to flow (into)

invidēns, -ntis: jealous

laedō, -ere, laesī, laesum: to wound

maximus, -a, -um: greatest, largest

optō (1): to desire

plūs: more (adv.)

plūs, plūris: more (adj.)

prīncipium, -ī n.: beginning, principle

quīcumque, quaecumque, quodcumque: any, whoever/whatever

sānctus, -a, -um: sacred; holy

secundus, -a, -um: following, second

similis, -e (+ gen. or dat.): similar

spīritus, -ūs m.: breath; spirit

testis, -is m.: witness

Aristotīle teste: *with Aristotle as our witness;* abl. absolute; the following phrases are from a *Liber Dē Causīs* translated from Arabic and believed (wrongly) to be by Aristotle; this formulation of the language is from Duns Scotus (*Quaestiōnēs Subtilissimae in Metaphysicam* Book 5 qu. 1)

quidquid est causa causae est causa causātī: *whatever is the cause of a cause is the cause of the thing caused;* the first cause is the cause of every other thing

Prīncipium...maximum dīcitur: *in any kind of thing whatsoever (in quōcumque genere), the foundation is said to be the greatest part;* Aristotle *Posterior Analytics* 2.13 (96b23–96b24); Foscarini reinforces his argument that Eve is responsible for Adam's sin by saying that the foundation is the most important part and therefore would take the responsibility for problems caused by what is on top of it

Et in *Posteriōribus*: propter quod ūnumquodque tāle et illud magis; sed propter Ēvam peccāvit Ādam, ergō multō magis peccāvit Ēva. Item sīcutī melius est bene facere quam bene patī, ita dēterius est male suādēre quam male suādērī; minus enim peccat, quī alterīus exemplō peccat, quia quod exemplō fit id quōdam iure fierī dīcitur. Ex quō vulgāre illud dīcī solet: "quod ā multīs peccātur inultum est."

dēterior, dēterius: worse (comp. adj.)

exemplum, -ī n.: example; precedent

inultus, -a, -um: unpunished, done with impunity

item: likewise

iūs, iūris n.: law

melius: better (comp. adv.)

minus: less (comp. adv.)

multō: by much (adv.)

Posterior, -ōris: Posterior Analytics

propter (+ acc.): on account of

sīcutī: just as

suādeō, -ēre, suāsī, suāsum: to persuade, urge

ūnusquisque, ūnaquaeque, ūnumquodque: each one

vulgāris, -e: usual, common

propter quod ūnumquodque tāle et illud magis: *on account of which thing each thing (is) such (as it is), (it is) also that thing more*; Aristotle *Posterior Analytics* 1.2 (79a29–30); it became a common scholastic saying

Item sīcutī melius...ita dēterius...: *Likewise just as it is better...so it is worse*; sīcutī corresponds to *ita*: "just as X...so Y"

bene facere quam bene patī: *to do good things rather than to have good things done to one*; literally "to do well rather than to fare well"

quia...fierī dīcitur: *because whatever is done with a precedent is said to be done with some right*

Ex quō: *From which (thing)*; the relative pronoun is referring to the idea of the previous clause

vulgāre illud dīcī solet: *there is the common saying*; literally, "that common thing is accustomed to be said," referring to the following quotation

quod ā multīs peccātur: *a sin that is committed by many*; quod peccātur is literally "that which is sinned"; the quotation is from Lucan *Dē Bellō Cīvīlī* 5.260

3.10 Et sī parī glōriā sē dignōs exīstimāssent, Ēva īnferior magis recessit ā mediō et per cōnsequēns magis accessit ad peccātum.

3.11 Facilius etiam potuit socia amīcissima virum dēcipere quam [197] turpissimus serpēns mulierem.

3.12 Longius etiam persevērāvit, quia prius coepit, et tantō graviōra sunt dēlicta (Gregōriī dēcrētō) quantō diūtius īnfēlīcem animam tenent alligātam.

---

accēdō, -ere, accessī, accessum: to approach
alligō (1): to bind
anima, -ae f.: soul
coepī, coepisse: to begin
cōnsequēns, -ntis n.: consequence
dēcernō, -ere, dēcrēvī, dēcrētum: to decide
dēcipiō, -ere, dēcēpī, dēceptum: to deceive
dēcrētum, -ī n.: doctrine, decree
dēlictum, -ī n.: offense
dignus, -a, -um (+ abl.): worthy
diū: (for) a long time
exīstimō (1): to think
facilius: more easily (comp. adv.)

glōria, -ae f.: glory
Gregōrius, -ī: Gregory the Great
īnfēlīx, īnfēlīcis: unhappy
īnferior, īnferius: worse, inferior
longius: longer (comp. adv.)
medium, -ī n.: the middle, mean
pār, paris: equal
persevērō (1): to persevere
prius: earlier, first (adv.)
quantō: (by) how much (adv.)
recēdō, -ere, recessī, recessum: to recede, depart
serpēns, -ntis: snake
socia, -ae f.: partner
tantō: (by) so much (adv.)
turpis, -e: disgraceful

---

quam turpissimus serpēns (potuit dēcipere) mulierem: *than the most disgraceful serpent (could deceive) the woman;* the verb *dēcipere* is carried over

tantō graviōra…quantō diūtius: *by so much graver…by however much longer;* that is, the longer a person has been in a sinful state, the more serious the offense

Gregōriī: *Gregory the Great;* a sixth-century pope; Foscarini here paraphrases from Gregory's *Liber Rēgulae Pastōrālis* 3.32 (*PL* 77.115)

3.13 Et, ut tandem mea conclūdātur ōrātiō, causa et exemplum peccātī fuit, et in exemplum vehementer Gregōrius culpam extendit. Et causam ignōrantium Iūdaeōrum, quia prīma fuit, magis damnāvit Chrīstus, quī errāre nōn poterat, quam sententiam Pīlātī doctiōris, cum dīxit: "Maius peccātum habent quī mē tibi trādidērunt etc."

Chrīstus, -ī m.: Christ
conclūdō, -ere, conclūsī, conclūsum: to conclude
culpa, -ae f.: blame
damnō (1): to condemn
doctus, -a, -um: learned, erudite
errō (1): to make a mistake
exemplum, -ī n.: example
extendō, -ere, extendī, extēnsum: to extend
Gregōrius, -ī m.: Gregory the Great
ignōrāns, -ntis: ignorant
ignōrō (1): to not know

Iūdaeī, -ōrum: Judeans; the Jewish people
maior, maius: greater (comp. adj.)
ōrātiō, -ōnis f.: speech
Pīlātus, -ī m.: Pontius Pilate, prefect of Judaea (26–36 CE)
sententia, -ae f.: opinion; sentence (judicial)
tandem: finally
trādō, -ere, trādidī, trāditum: to hand over
vehementer: forcefully

---

in exemplum...culpam extendit: *he extends guilt to the example;* the idea is from Gregory's *Liber Rēgulae Pastōrālis* 1.2 (*PL* 77.15–16)
ignōrantium Iūdaeōrum: *of the ignorant Jews;* an antisemitic epithet; for more on antisemitism in the *Defense of Eve*, see Introduction IV
Pīlātī doctiōris: *of the quite learned Pilate;* Pontius Pilate was the Roman prefect who ordered the crucifixion of Jesus
"Maius peccātum habent quī mē tibi trādidērunt etc.": *they who handed me over to you have sinned more etc.";* a paraphrase John 19:11, where the verb is singular, perhaps referring to Caiaphas, the chief Judean official who handed Jesus over to Pilate for punishment

Cui sententiae acquiēscendum omnēs, quī Chrīstiānī nūncupārī voluēre, putāvērunt, tū vērō Chrīstiānissima ipsam ratiōnibus comprobābis.

3.14 Valē et nē timeās et audē multa, quia plūrima optimē didicistī et doctissimē scrībis!

4.1 Rēspōnsiō Isōtae: Dēcrēveram mē tēcum amplius nōn [198] inīre certāmen, quia, ut inquis, mea castra meīs iaculīs oppugnās.

---

acquiēscō, -ere, acquiēvī, acquiētum: to agree

amplius: further, more fully (comp. adv.)

audeō, -ēre, ausus sum: to dare

certāmen, -inis n.: contest, dispute

Chrīstiānus, -a, -um: Christian

comprobō (1): to approve, confirm

dēcernō, -ere, dēcrēvī, dēcrētum: to decide

discō, -ere, didicī, -: to learn

doctus, -a, -um: learned, erudite

iaculum, -ī n.: spear; weapon

ineō, -īre, -īvī, -itum: to enter; undertake

Isōta, -ae f.: Isotta (Nogarola)

nūncupō (1): to call

oppugnō (1): to attack, fight

plūrimus, -a, -um: very many

ratiō, -ōnis f.: reason

rēspōnsiō, -ōnis f.: response

scrībō, -ere, scrīpsī, scrīptum: to write

sententia, -ae f.: opinion

valeō, -ēre, -uī: to be well; goodbye (imperative)

vērō: but, and (postpositive)

Cui sententiae acquiēscendum (esse): *that there must be agreement with this opinion;* there is an implied *esse* forming an indirect statement set up by *putāvērunt*

quī...voluēre: *who have wished to be called Christian; voluēre = voluērunt*

Valē: *Goodbye;* a standard ending for a letter

nē timeās: *do not fear;* negative jussive subjunctive

Dēcrēveram mē...certāmen: *I had decided not to undertake a contest with you;* indirect statement

ut inquis: *as you say;* referring to Foscarini's words in 3.1

Ita ea quae ad mē dedistī perfectō et solertī studiō disputāta sunt, ut eīs obicī nōn ā mē sed ā quibusvīs doctissimīs virīs difficillimum sit. Vērum cum hoc certāmen ūtile mihi esse cognōscam, dēcrēvī huic tuae honestae voluntātī mōrem gerere; licet autem incassum certāre cognōscam, tamen mihi summa laus erit ā tē virō fortissimō superārī.

---

certāmen, -inis, n.: contest, dispute
certō (1): to compete; to dispute
cognōscō, -ere, cognōvī, cognitum: to recognize
dēcernō, -ere, dēcrēvī, dēcrētum: to decide
difficilis, -e: difficult
disputō (1): discuss, debate, argue
doctus, -a, -um: learned, erudite
fortis, -e: strong
honestus, -a, -um: honorable
incassum: in vain; uselessly (adv.)
laus, laudis f.: praise; a source of praise

licet (+ subj.) although
obiciō, -ere, obiēcī, obiectum (+ dat.): to throw against, oppose
perfectus, -a, -um: perfect, complete
quīvīs, quaevīs, quodvīs: whoever, whatever
solers, -tis: skilled (= CL sollers, -tis)
studium, -ī n.: zeal, study
summus, -a, -um: highest
superō (1): to conquer, overcome
ūtilis, -e: useful
vērum: but (conjunction)
voluntās, -tātis f.: will, desire

---

ea quae ad mē dedistī: *the (arguments) which you sent to me;* literally "which you gave"; *dare* is the typical verb used for sending letters

ut eīs...difficillimum sit: *such that it would be difficult for them to be objected to by not only myself but by any educated man;* a result clause wherein *obicī* is the predicate of *sit* which takes *difficillimum* as a subject

cum hoc...cognōscam: *because I recognize;* causal *cum*-clause

mōrem gerere: *to do as you wish;* Nogarola used the same idiom in 2.6 to again emphasize that she was writing only at Foscarini's insistence

incassum certāre cognōscam: *I know (myself) to compete (with you) in vain;* indirect statement

mihi summa laus...superārī: *it will be the highest honor for me to be overcome by so strong a man as you;* there is a flirtatious edge to the banter, as above when she jokes about him "storming (her) castle" (*mea castra...oppugnās*)

58

4.2 Ēva ignōrāns incōnstānsque peccāvit, ex quō tibi gravius peccāsse vidētur, quia ignōrantia eōrum quae scīre dēbēmus nōs nōn excūsat, quia scrīptum est "Ignōrāns ignōrābitur." Concēdō, cum haec ignōrantia crassa fuerit vel affectāta, sed ignōrantia Ēvae ā nātūrā fuit īnsita, cuius nātūrae ipse Deus est auctor et conditor.

affectō (1): to pretend
auctor, -ōris m.: author; source
concēdō, -ere, concēssī, concēssum: to concede
conditor, -ōris m.: creator
crassus, -a, -um: thick, gross
excūsō (1): to excuse, justify
ignōrāns, -ntis: ignorant

ignōrantia, -ae f.: ignorance
ignōrō (1): to not know; be ignorant
inconstans, -ntis: changeable, inconstant
īnserō, -ere, īnsēvī, īnsitum: to insert, implant
scrībō, -ere, scrīpsī, scrīptum: to write
vel: or; even, actually

ex quō…vidētur: *from which thing she seemed to you to sin more gravely;* antecedent of *quō* is understood to be the fact that Eve sinned from ignorance and inconstancy
gravius: *more gravely;* comparative adverb
peccāsse: *to have sinned;* syncopated form of *peccāvisse*
"Ignōrāns ignōrābitur": *"Anyone ignoring (this) will be ignored";* 1 Cor.14:38, as noted above (3.2), Paul writes that anyone who believes women should be allowed to speak in church should be ignored
Concēdō: *I concede (that this is true)*
cum haec ignōrantia…vel affectāta: *when this ignorance has been excessive or pretended;* Nogarola means to say that Foscarini is correct only about ignorance for which the person in question is ultimately responsible
fuit īnsita: *was implanted;* perfect passive (= CL *est īnsita*)

Nam in plūribus hoc vidētur, quia quī plūs ignōrat [199] minus peccat, ut puer sene, rūsticus nōbilī; ad quem salvandum nōn expedit ut ea sciat quae pertinent ad salūtem explicitē, sed implicitē, quia sōla fidēs sufficit.

4.3 Parī etiam gressū ratiō incōnstantiae prōcēdit. Et cum dīcitur "Dē incōnstantiā vērō prōcēdentēs operātiōnēs vituperābiliōrēs sunt," intelligitur dē incōnstantiā quae nōn est secundum nātūram,

expediō, -īre, -īvī, -ītum: to be advantageous, useful, convenient
explicitē: explicitly
gressus, -ūs m.: step; progression
ignōrō (1): to not know; be ignorant
implicitē: implicitly
inconstāns, -ntis: changeable, fickle
inconstantia, -ae f.: inconstancy, fickleness
intelligō, -ere, intellēxī, intellēxum: to understand; realize
minor, minus: less (comp. adj.)
minus: less (comp. adv.)
nōbilis, -e: noble
operātiō, -ōnis f.: action
pār, paris: equal

pertineō, -ēre, -uī: to reach; extend; relate to
plūs: more (comp. adv.)
plūs, plūris: more (comp. adj.)
prōcēdō, -ere, prōcessī, prōcessum: to proceed
ratiō, -ōnis f.: reason; rationale
rūsticus, -ī m.: peasant, farmer
salūs, -ūtis f.: salvation
salvō (1): to save
secundum (+ acc.): in accordance with
senex, -is m.: old man
sufficiō, -ere, suffēcī, suffectum: to be sufficient
vērō: but, and (postpositive)
vituperābilis, -e: blameworthy

Nam in plūribus hoc vidētur: *For this is seen in many (instances)*
ut puer sene, rūsticus nōbilī: *as the boy (sins less) than the old man, the peasant (sins less) than the noble;* the verb *minus peccat* is implied for both; the second element of each is an abl. of comparison
ad quem salvandum: *for whom to be saved;* ad + gerundive phrase to express purpose
Et cum dīcitur: *And when it is said;* what follows is a quote from Foscarini in 3.3
intelligitur (esse) dē incōnstantiā: *it is understood (to be) concerning inconstancy which…;* there is an implied *esse* as a complementary infinitive to *intelligitur*

sed secundum mōrēs et vitia.

4.4 Similiter dē imperfectiōne: "Cum enim augentur dōna, ratiōnēs etiam crēscunt dōnōrum." Deus cum hominem creāvit, ab initiō creāvit illum perfectum et animae eius potentiās perfectās, et dēdit eī maiōrem vēritātis ratiōnem et cognitiōnem, maiōrem quoque sapientiae profunditātem, ita ut dominus addūceret cūncta animantia terrae et volātilia caelī ad Ādam, ut ea suīs nōminibus [200] appellāret.

---

addūcō, -ere, addūxī, adductum: to lead (to someone)

anima, -ae f.: soul

animō (1): to be alive

appellō (1): to call by name

augeō, -ēre, auxī, auctum: to augment

cognitiō, -ōnis f.: knowledge

creō (1): to create

crēscō, -ere, crēvī, crētum: to increase

cūnctus, -a, -um: all

dōnum, -ī n.: gift

imperfectiō, -ōnis f.: imperfection

initium, -ī n.: beginning

maior, maius: greater (comp. adj.)

perfectus, -a, -um: perfect, complete

potentia, -ae f.: power

profunditās, -tātis f.: depth

ratiō, -ōnis f.: reason; reasoning

sapientia, -ae f.: wisdom

secundum (+ acc.): in accordance with

similiter: similarly

vēritās, -tātis f.: truth

vitium, -ī n.: sin; character defect

volātilis, -e: flying

---

dē imperfectiōne: *concerning imperfection;* Nogarola here rebuts an argument about imperfection, yet Foscarini did not make such an argument; it could be that they later removed the argument (see Introduction IX)

ratiōnēs etiam crēscunt dōnōrum: *the rationale of the gifts furthermore increases;* reason is understood to mean responsibility; the quotation is from Gregory the Great, *Homilies on the Gospels* 9 (*PL* 76.1106)

ita ut: *to such an extent that...;* begins a result clause which paraphrases Gen. 2:19–20

cūncta animantia: *all the animals;* literally "all the living things", *animantia* being the participle of *animāre*

volātilia caelī: *the flying things of the sky;* birds

ut ea...appellāret: *so that he (Adam) could call them by their names;* purpose clause

Unde dīxit: "Faciāmus hominem ad imāginem et similitūdinem nostram, et praesit piscibus maris et volātilibus caelī et bēstiīs terrae ūniversaeque creātūrae," dēnotāns ipsīus perfectiōnem. Dē muliere vērō dīxit: "Nōn est bonum hominem esse sōlum, faciāmus eī adiūtōrium simile sibi."

adiūtōrium, -ī n.: help, aid
bēstia, -ae f.: beast, animal
creātūra, -ae f.: creation
creō (1): to create
dēnotō (1): to indicate
imāgō, -inis f.: image
perfectiō, -ōnis f.: perfection, completion
piscis, -is m.: fish

praesum, praeesse, praefuī, praefuturum (+ dat.): to be in charge of
similis, -e (+ gen. or dat.): similar
similitūdō, -inis f.: likeness
unde: from where, from which thing, that's why
ūniversus, -a, -um: whole, entire
vērō: but, and (postpositive)
volātilis, -e: flying

Unde dīxit (Deus): *That's why he (God) said*
"Faciāmus hominem...creātūrae": *"Let us make man in our image and likeness so he may rule the fish of the sea and the birds of the sky, the beasts of the earth, all of the creation";* a quotation from Gen. 1:26 in which *Faciāmus* and *praesit* are jussive subjunctives
dēnotāns ipsīus perfectiōnem: *indicating the perfection of (Adam) himself*
dīxit (Deus): (*God) said...;* the following quote is from Gen. 2:18; Nogarola argues that while Adam was created in God's image to rule creation, woman was less perfect because she was created only to provide Adam someone like himself as a helper
Nōn est bonum: *It is not good;* the phrase sets up an indirect statement, *hominem esse sōlum* ("that man be alone")

Et quia beātitūdō est cum cōnsōlātiōne et gaudiō, sōlātium autem et gaudium nōn potest quis habēre sōlus, vidētur quod Deus eam creāvit ad virī cōnsōlātiōnem, quia "bonum est suī ipsīus diffusīvum," et quantō maius tantō magis sē commūnicat. Ergō maius vidētur peccātum Ādae. Ambrosius: "Quō indulgentior līberālitās, eō inexcūsābilior est pervicācia."

Ambrosius, -ī m.: Ambrose (fourth-century bishop)

beatitūdō, -is f.: happiness

commūnicō (1): to share, make common

cōnsōlātiō, -ōnis f.: consolation, comfort

creō (1): to create

diffundō, -ere, diffūdī, diffūsus: to diffuse, spread

eō: by that much (adv.)

gaudium, -ī n.: joy

inexcūsābilis, -e: inexcusable

līberālitās, -tātis f.: generosity

maior, maius: greater (comp. adj.)

pervicācia, -ae f.: stubbornness, obstinacy

quantō: by however much

sōlātium, -ī n.: solace, relief

tantō: by so much (adv.)

sōlātium: *solace;* an alternate spelling for *sōlācium*

nōn potest (ali)quis habēre sōlus: *nor is anyone alone able to have;* the *ali-* drops out from the *aliquis* after the negation

vidētur quod Deus...virī cōnsōlātiōnem: *it seems that God created her (Eve) for the consolation of man (Adam);* this indirect statement started by *quod* establishes Eve's inferiority which Nogarola will interpret as lessened responsibility

bonum est suī...sē commūnicat.: *good is diffusive of itself, and the greater (the good) is, the more it shares itself;* a neoplatonic idea discussed by Thomas Aquinas (*Summa Theologica* Book I qu. 5 art. 4), which Nogarola uses here to suggest that Eve existed to have Adam's goodness imposed upon her

Ambrosius (scrībit): "Quō...pervicācia": *Ambrose (writes): "By however much the generosity is more indulgent, by this much the stubbornness is more inexcusable";* quotation from Ambrose (fourth century) *Expositiō in Lūcam* 9.23 (*PL* 15.1891), which repeats a sentiment from 4.2 that those who are superior have higher expectations

4.5 "Cūstōdia autem Ādae commissa sociam nōn excūsat, quia fūrēs, quōrum operā paterfamiliās cōnfīdēns ūtitur, ultimō suppliciō nōn pūniuntur, velutī extrāneī et illī dē quibus nūlla est habita cōnfīdentia." Vērum est hoc in lēgibus temporālibus, sed nōn in [201] dīvīnīs; nam iūstitia dīvīna aliter in pūniendō prōcēdit quam temporālis.

---

aliter: otherwise

committō, -ere, -īvī, -issum: to commit, entrust

cōnfīdentia, -ae f.: confidence

cōnfīdō, -ere, cōnfīsus sum: to be confident of; to believe

cūstōdia, -ae f.: protection

dīvīnus, -a, -um: divine

excūsō (1): to excuse, justify

extrāneus, -ī m.: outsider

familia, -ae f.: family; household

fūr, fūris m.: thief

iūstitia, -ae f.: justice

lēx, lēgis f.: law

opera, -ae f.: work, labor

prōcēdō, -ere, prōcessī, prōcessum: to proceed

pūniō, -īre, pūnīvī, pūnītum: to punish

socia, -ae f.: partner, companion (female)

supplicium, -ī n.: punishment

temporālis, -e: secular

ultimus, -a, -um: final; ultimate

ūtor, utī, ūsus sum (+ abl.): to use; employ

velutī: just as

vērum: but (conjunction)

"Cūstōdia autem...est habita cōnfīdentia": Foscarini had written this in 3.4

fūrēs, quōrum operā...cōnfīdēns ūtitur: *thieves, whose work the head of a household trustingly employs;* ūtitur takes the ablative *operā*

paterfamiliās: *the head of the household;* a technical term that combines *pater* and *familiās*, which is the archaic genitive of *familia*

ultimō suppliciō nōn pūniuntur: *thieves are not punished with the most severe punishment;* suppliciō is in the ablative of means

velutī extrāneī...habita cōnfīdentia: *just as strangers and those from whom no confidence is maintained [are punished];* pūniuntur is the implied verb for *extrāneī* and *illī, dē* takes the ablative *quibus,* and *cōnfīdentia* agrees with *nūlla*

Vērum est..nōn in dīvīnīs: *But this is in secular laws, not in divine ones;* the *vērum* could also be interpreted as a neuter adjective agreeing with *hoc* ("This is true...")

4.6 "Fragilitās etiam mulieris nōn fuit peccātī causa, sed inōrdinātus appetītus appetendī id quod nātūrae suae nōn competēbat" — quod prōcēdit, ut scrībis, ex superbiā. Minus tamen peccātum vidētur scientiam appetere bonī et malī, quam trānsgrediendī praeceptum dīvīnum, quia appetītus sciendī est quoddam nātūrāle et "omnēs hominēs ā nātūrā scīre dēsīderant."

appetītus, -ūs m.: appetite
appetō, -ere, -īvī, -ītum: to strive after
competō, -ere, competīvī,
competītum: to be suitable for
dēsīderō (1): to desire
dīvīnus, -a, -um: divine
fragilitās, -tātis f.: frailty, weakness
inōrdinātus, -a, -um: inordinate,
excessive
minor, minus: smaller (comp. adj.)

nātūra, -ae: nature
praeceptum, -ī n.: command
prōcēdō, -ere, -essī, -essum: to
proceed
scientia, -ae f.: knowledge
scrībō, -ere, scrīpsī, scrīptum: to write
superbia, -ae f.: arrogance
trānsgredior, -edī, -essus sum: to
violate

"Fragilitās etiam...nōn competēbat": "*In addition, the weakness of woman was not the cause of sin, but rather an inordinate appetite for seeking that which was not fit for her nature*"; Nogarola paraphrases Foscarini's argument from 3.5

Minus tamen peccātum vidētur: *However it seems a smaller sin; minus* here is a neuter adjective modifying *peccātum*, rather than adverb

scientiam...bonī et malī: *knowledge...of good and evil;* the *scientiam* is the object of *appetere*; the adjectives *bonī et malī* are acting substantively as abstract nouns

quam (peccātum) trānsgrediendī praeceptum dīvīnum: *than (the sin) of transgressing a divine command;* gerund here governing a direct object in the acc.

appetītus sciendī: *an appetite for knowing;* the *sciendī* is an objective gen.

quoddam nātūrāle: *something natural;* literally "a certain natural thing"; *nātūrāle* is acting substantively

"omnēs...dēsīderant": *"all humans by nature desire to know"*; Aristotle *Metaphysics* 1.1 (980α); Nogarola argues that Eve's desire for knowledge is natural to all humans and not an appetite inappropriate for her status

Et licet prīmus mōtus fuerit appetītus inōrdinātus, quī sine peccātō esse nōn potest, tamen tolerābilius est quam trānsgressiōnis peccātum; nam mandātōrum observantia est via quā ītur ad salūtis patriam: "Sī vīs ad vītam ingredī, servā [202] mandāta." Item: "Quid faciendō vītam aeternam possidēbō? Servā mandāta." Et trānsgressiō propriē orītur ex superbiā,

aeternus, -a, -um: eternal

appetītus, -ūs m.: appetite

appetō, -ēre, -īvī, -ītum: to strive after

ingredior, ingredī, ingressus sum: to advance to, enter, approach

inōrdinātus, -a, -um: inordinate, excessive

item: likewise

licet (+ subj.): although

mandātum, -ī n.: command

mōtus, -ūs m.: movement, motion, impulse

orior, orīrī, ortus sum: to arise

patria, -ae f.: fatherland

possideō, -ēre, possēdī, possessum: to possess

propriē: particularly

salūs, salūtis f.: health; salvation

servō (1): keep, maintain

superbia, -ae f.: arrogance

tolerābilior, -ius: more tolerable (comp. adj.)

trānsgressiō, -ōnis f.: transgression

---

prīmus mōtus (peccātī) fuerit appetītus inōrdinātus: *the first impetus (of sin) was an inordinate appetite;* Nogarola argues that while Eve's eating the fruit set the original sin in motion, the sin of seeking knowledge is less than the sin of transgressing a divine command

tolerābilius (peccātum): *a more tolerable (sin)*

ītur: *one goes;* impersonal passive

Sī vīs...mandāta: *If you want to enter into life, keep the commandments;* Matthew 19:17

"Quid faciendō ... mandāta": *What should I do to attain eternal life? Keep the commandments;* the gerund *faciendō* is an abl. of means with *quid* as its object ("by doing what thing"); versions of this statement appear in Matthew 19:17, Mark 10:17, and Luke 18:18

quia superbia nihil aliud est quam rēgulae dīvīnae nōlle subiicī, quam extollere sē suprā id quod secundum rēgulam dīvīnam praefīxum est Deī voluntātem contemnendō et suam adimplendō. Item Augustīnus *Dē Nātūrā et Grātiā*: "Peccātum est voluntās cōnsequendī vel retinendī quod iūstitia vetat," id est nōlle quod Deus vult. Cui concordāt Ambrosius in librō *Dē Paradīsō*:

adimpleō, -ēre, -ēvī, -ētum: to fill up
Ambrosius, -ī m.: Ambrose (fourth-century bishop)
Augustīnus, -ī m.: Augustine (fourth/fifth-century bishop)
concordō (1): to agree
cōnsequor, cōnsequī, cōnsecūtus sum: to follow; obtain
contemnō, -ere, contempsī, contemptum: to scorn
dīvīnus, -a, -um: divine
extollō, extollere: to elevate
grātia, -ae f.: grace
item: likewise
iūstitia, -ae f.: justice

nātūra, -ae f.: nature
nōlō, nōlle, nōluī: to be unwilling
paradīsus, -ī m.: paradise
praefīgō, -ere, praefīxī, praefīxum: to set in front
rēgula, -ae f.: rule
retineo, -ēre, retinuī, retentum: to retain
secundum (+acc): according to
sūbiiciō, sūbicere, sūbiecī, sūbiectum (+ dat.): to submit
superbia, -ae f.: arrogance
suprā (+acc): above
vetō, vetāre, vetuī, vetītum: to forbid
voluntās, -tātis f.: desire, will

superbia nihil aliud est quam: *arrogance is nothing other than*
rēgulae dīvīnae nōlle subiicī: *to be unwilling to be subjected to divine rule;* the *subiicī* is a passive infinitive set up by *nōlle*
quam extollere sē: *than to elevate oneself;* coordinated with above *quam* in asyndeton
Deī voluntātem...suam (voluntātem): *God's will...one's own (will);* these accusatives are the direct objects of *contemnendō* and *adimplendō* respectively
Dē Nātūrā et Grātiā: Augustine does make similar statements in *On Nature and Grace* ch. 67 (*PL* 44.286–288), but the exact quotation is from *Dē Duābus Animābus* 11.15 (*PL* 42.105)
Dē Paradīsō: the quotation is from *On Paradise* 8.39 (*PL* 14.292), as found in Thomas Aquinas (*Summa Theologica* Book IIa q.100 a.2)

"Peccātum est trānsgressiō dīvīnae lēgis et caelestium inoboedientia mandātōrum." Ecce quia trānsgressiō et inoboedientia caelestium mandātōrum est maximum peccātum, cum peccātī sit ista dēfīnītiō: "Peccātum est inōrdinātus appetītus sciendī." Ergō maius vidētur peccātum trānsgressiōnis praeceptī quam bonī et malī scientiam appetere;

appetītus, -ūs m.: appetite
appetō, -ēre, -īvī, -ītum: to strive after
caelestis, -e: heavenly
dēfīnītiō, -ōnis f.: definition
dīvīnus, -a, -um: divine
ecce: look!
inoboedientia, -ae f.: disobedience

inōrdinātus, -a, -um: inordinate, excessive
lēx, lēgis f.: law
maior, maius: greater (comp. adj.)
mandātum, -ī n.: command
praeceptum, -ī n.: command
scientia, -ae f.: knowledge
trānsgressiō, -ōnis f.: transgression

trānsgressiō dīvīnae lēgis...caelestium inoboedientia mandātōrum: *transgression of divine law...disobedience to the heavenly commands;* objective gen. in both cases

Ecce quia: *Look at the fact that; quia* here introduces a noun clause

cum peccātī sit ista dēfīnītiō: *although your definition of sin is (the following);* concessive *cum*-clause; the *ista dēfīnītiō* is literally "that definition of yours," referring to Foscarini's argument in 3.5

maius...quam: *greater...than;* comparing the sins of transgressing heavenly commands and seeking knowledge

peccātum trānsgressiōnis praeceptī: *sin of transgression of a command;* both genitives are objective

bonī et malī scientiam: *knowledge of good and evil;* the adjectives are substantive, acting as abstract nouns

— [203] licet inōrdinātē appetere sit peccātum, sīcut in Ēvā, quae tamen nōn appetīvit sē esse Deō similem in potentiā, sed in scientiā tantum bonī et malī, secundum quod sibi erat etiam ā nātūrā persuāsum.

4.7 Quod autem verba illa ("Sī Ādam nōn peccāsset") tē in sententiā cōnfirmant quia ita fortasse peccāvit Ēva ut nōn meruerit redēmptiōnem velutī daemonēs, dīcō quod et ipsa cum Ādam redēmpta fuit,

---

appetō, -ēre, -īvī, -ītum: to strive after
cōnfirmō (1): to confirm; strengthen
daemōn, -onis m.: demon
fortasse: perhaps
inōrdinātus, -a, -um: inordinate, excessive
licet (+ subj.): although
mereō, -ēre, meruī, meritum: to earn
persuādeō, -ēre, persuāsī, persuāsum: to persuade

potentia, -ae f.: power
redēmptiō, -ōnis f.: redemption
redimō, -ere, redēmī, redēmptum: to redeem
scientia, -ae f.: knowledge
secundum (+ acc.): in accordance with
sententia, -ae f.: opinion
sīcut: just as
similis, -e (+ gen. or dat.): similar
velutī: just as

---

quae tamen:: *who nevertheless;* the antecedent is Eve

in scientiā tantum: *in knowledge only;* the *tantum* here is the adv. "only"

quod sibi...persuāsum: *that which she had been persuaded to do;* literally "that which had been persuaded to her"; *persuāsum* is an impersonal passive because the verb *persuādēre* is intransitive and so cannot take a personal subject in the passive

Quod autem verba illa...cōnfirmant: *As to the fact that those words...confirm;* noun clause

"Sī Ādam nōn peccāsset": *"If Adam had not sinned";* Nogarola is referring to Foscarini's response (3.6) to her own argument about these words (2.4)

ut nōn meruerit: *that she did not earn;* perf. subj. because it is a result clause

dīcō quod et ipsa... redēmpta fuit: *I say that even she herself was redeemed;* the indirect statement uses *quod* + indicative, as often in post-classical Latin; *redēmpta fuit* = CL *redēmpta est*

quia "os ex ossibus meīs et carō dē carne meā." Et sī Deus eam appārenter nōn redēmit, hoc fuit indubiē quia Deus prō nihilō peccātum illīus aestimāvit. Nam sī redēmptiōnem meruit homō, multō magis mulier propter dēlictī parvitātem. Nam in angelō nōn fuit per ignōrantiam excūsātiō, sīcut in muliere; angelus enim sine [204] inquīsītiōne et discursū intelligit,

aestimō (1): to estimate; to value

angelus, -ī m.: angel

appārenter: in appearance only (adv.)

carō, carnis f.: flesh

dēlictum, -ī n.: fault

discursus, -ūs m.: discourse

excūsātiō, -ōnis f.: excuse

ignōrantia, -ae f.: ignorance

indubiē: undoubtedly

inquīsītiō, -ōnis f.: searching, asking

intelligō, -ere, intellēxī, -ēctum: to understand

mereō, -ēre, meruī, meritum: to earn

multō: by much (adv.)

nihilum, -ī n.: nothing

os, ossis n.: bone

parvitās, -tātis f.: smallness; insignificance

propter (+ acc.): on account of

redēmptiō, -ōnis f.: redemption

sīcut: just as

"os...meā": *"bone from my bones and flesh from my flesh"*; Genesis 2:23

sī Deus...nōn redēmit: *if God seems to have not redeemed Eve;* that is, if God did not redeem Eve, it would have been in appearances only; God did not forgive Eve because he believed her sin was so negligible as to not require forgiveness

peccātum illīus: *the sin of that man (Adam);* God valued Adam's sin at nothing, since he still redeemed Adam; therefore Eve must have been redeemed, since her sin was less serious than Adam's

in angelō...excūsātiō: *in the case of the angel, there was no excuse (that he had done it) through ignorance*; the angel here is Lucifer, who rose up against God; Nogarola will argue that while Eve wanted god-like knowledge, Lucifer could only have risen up to take god-like power since he already had god-like knowledge (and therefore did not have the "excuse through ignorance")

70

et intellēctum habet magis deiformem quam homō, cui similem dīcī potest Ēva appetīsse. Unde angelus dīcitur intellēctuālis et homō ratiōnālis, et ubi mulier ex appetītū scientiae, angelus peccāvit ex appetītū potentiae. Modo omnimoda vīsiōnis scientia potest creātūrae commūnicārī, sed nōn omnimoda potentia Deī et animae Chrīstī.

angelus, -ī m.: angel	**modo**: only (adv.)
anima, -ae f.: soul, spirit	**omnimodus, -a, -um**: every kind;
appetītus, -ūs m.: appetite	complete
appetō, -ēre, -īvī, -ītum: to seek	**potentia, -ae f.**: power
Chrīstus, -ī m.: Christ	**ratiōnālis, -e**: rational
communicō (1): to communicate	**scientia, -ae f.**: knowledge
creātūra, -ae: creation	**similis, -e (+gen. or dat.)**: similar
creō (1): to create	**unde**: from where, from which point,
deifōrmis, -e: god-like	that's why
intellēctuālis, -e: intellectual	**vīsiō, -ōnis f.**: vision
intellēctus, -ūs: understanding	

cui similem dīcī potest Ēva appetīsse: *to which Eve can be said to have sought (to be) similar; cuī* is in dative with *simile; appetīsse* the syncopated form of *appetīvisse*

angelus...intellēctuālis et homō ratiōnālis: *the angel intellectual and humankind rational;* technical terms, "intellectual" here is the ability to understand without asking or speaking, while "rational" is to ability to reason things through discourse

ex appetītū scientiae...potentiae: *from an appetite for knowledge...power;* Eve's sin differs from the devil's because Eve was seeking god-like knowledge, whereas Lucifer, who already had god-like knowledge, could only have been seeking power

omnimoda vīsiōnis scientia: *complete knowledge of vision;* the "knowledge of vision" (*scientia vīsiōnis*) is a technical term in scholastic Latin for God's knowledge of all things based on his ability to simultaneously see the past, present, and future (Aquinas *Summa Theologica* Book I q.14 a.9)

creātūrae commūnicārī: *to be shared with a creation;* literally, "to be communicated (*commūnicārī*) to a creation (*creātūrae*)"

Item mulier peccāns dē veniā cōgitāvit, crēdēns illud utique esse peccātum, sed nōn tantum quod dēbēret Deus tālem īnferre sententiam et poenam; angelus autem nōn cōgitāvit. Unde Gregōrius IIII.° *Mōrālium*: "Prīmī parentēs ad hoc requīsītī sunt, ut peccātum quod trānsgrediendō commīserant cōnfitendō dēlērent; unde serpēns ille persuāsor, quia nōn erat revocandus ad veniam, nōn est dē culpā requīsītus."

angelus, -ī m.: angel
cōgitō (1): to think
committō, -ere, commissī, commissum: to commit
cōnfiteor, cōnfitērī, cōnfessus sum: to confess
dēlēo, -ēre, -ēvī, -ētum: to destroy; remove
Gregōrius, -ī m.: Gregory (the Great)
īnferō, īnferre, intulī, inlātum: to inflict, impose
item: likewise
mōrālis, -e: moral

persuasor, -ōris: persuador
requīrō, -ere, requīsīvī, requīsītum: to seek; question
revocō (1): to recall
sententia, -ae f.: opinion, sentence (judicial)
serpēns, -ntis m.: serpent, snake
tālis, tāle: such; distinguished
trānsgredior, trānsgredī, trānsgressus sum: to violate
unde: from where, from which thing
utique: certainly
venia, -ae f.: pardon, forgiveness

tantum quod dēbēret Deus...īnferre: *(a sin) so great that God would...inflict;* a result clause beginning with *quod* rather than *ut*
Unde Gregōrius IIII.° *Mōrālium*: *That's why Gregory (says) in fourth book of Mōrālia;* this statement is similar to one in *Mōrālia* 4.36.62 (*PL* 75.671), but it more closely follows the words of Gratian *Dē Penitentiā* 1.563–66, about the rite of confession
Prīmī parentēs...dēlērent: *"The first parents were questioned for this (reason), so that the sin they had committed by transgressing they could erase by confessing";* the first parents are Adam and Eve, who will receive a pardon by confessing their sin, which in turn implies that their sins are not unforgivable
unde...requīsītus: *That's why that serpent, that famous persuador, because he was not to be recalled to forgiveness, was not asked of his fault;* the serpent's sin was unforgivable, and that is why he was not questioned by God like Adam and Eve

Ergō [205] vidētur Ēva magis meruisse redēmptiōnem quam daemonēs.

4.8 Quod autem mulier omnēs poenās virī et ipsa patiātur, et ultrā ea quae commūnia sunt, sōla parit cum dolōre et virō subdita est, etiam haec mē in sententiā cōnfirmant, quia, ut dīxī, "omne bonum est suī ipsīus diffūsīvum," et quantō maius tantō magis sē commūnicat.

---

commūnicō (1): to share
commūnis, -e: common, shared
cōnfirmō (1): to confirm, strengthen
culpa, -ae f.: fault
daemōn, -onis m.: demon
diffūsīvus, -a, -um: diffusive
maior, maius: greater (comp. adj.)
mereō, -ēre, meruī, meritum: to earn
pariō, parere, peperī, partum: to give birth

quantō: (by) how much (adv.)
redēmptiō, -ōnis f.: redemption
requīrō, -ere, requīsīvī, requīsītum: to seek, question
sententia, -ae f.: opinion
subdō, -ere, subdidī, subditum: to subject, subordinate
tantō: (by) so much (adv.)
ultrā (+ acc.): beyond

Quod…patiātur: *As to the fact that the woman…endured;* a noun clause with a subjunctive of reported reason; Nogarola is referring back to Foscarini's argument in 3.7
sōla…virō subdita est: *since she alone gives birth in pain and has been subordinated to the man;* Genesis 3:16
ut dīxī: *as I said;* see above 4.4, with commentary
"omne bonum est…diffūsīvum": *every good is diffusive of itself;* good things by nature spread their goodness to others, a neoplatonic idea discussed by Thomas Aquinas (*Summa Theologica* Book I qu.5 a.4)
quantō maius (bonum est) tantō magis sē commūnicat: *by how much greater (the good is), by that much more it shares itself*

Ita et malum quantō maius, tantō magis sē commūnicat, et quantō magis sē commūnicat, tantō magis nocet, et quantō magis nocet, tantō maius est. Item secundum mēnsūram dēlictī erit et plāgārum modus. Unde Chrīstus voluit in cruce morī, licet turpissimum et atrōcissimum genus mortis fuerit, in quā sustinuit generāliter omnēs passiōnēs secundum genus.

atrōx, -ōcis: atrocious
Chrīstus, -ī m.: Christ
commūnicō (1): to share, make common
crux, crucis f.: cross
dēlictum, -tī n.: sin
generāliter: generally, in general
item: also, similarly
licet (+ subj): although
maior, maius: greater (comp. adj.)
mēnsūra, -ae f.: measure
morior, morī, mortuus sum: to die

noceō, -ēre, nocuī, nocitum: to harm
passiō, -ōnis f.: suffering (esp. of Christ)
plāga, -ae f.: strike; misfortune
quantō: (by) how much
secundum (+ acc.): according to
sustineō, -ēre, sustinuī, sustentum: to bear, endure
turpis, -e: shameful
unde: from which place, for this reason, that's why

Ita et malum…: *In the same way, evil too…* ; Nogrola puts forward a progression of three steps: the greater evil is the more it spreads, and the more it spreads the more it harms, and the more it harms the greater it is; this progression buttresses her argument that Adam's sin caused more harm, and therefore was a greater sin than Eve's

secundum…modus: *the measure of the misfortunes will be according to the measure of the crime;* a small sin should have a small punishment, while a large sin should have a large punishment; Nogarola will argue that Adam's sin caused Christ's suffering

voluit in cruce morī: *voluntarily died on the cross;* the verb *velle* can have a sense of "to do something voluntarily"

generāliter: *in general;* that is, suffering for all of humanity in general

Unde Īsidōrus *Dē Trīnitāte*: "Ūnigenitus Deī filius ad peragendum mortis suae sacrāmentum cōnsummāsse sē omne genus passiōnum testātur, cum inclīnātō capite ēmīsit spīritum." Ratiō: quia poena dēbēbat [206] culpae correspondēre. Ādam tulit pōmum lignī vetitī, Chrīstus passus est in lignō et sīc satisfēcit.

Chrīstus, -ī m.: Christ
cōnsummō (1): to bring together, unite
correspondeō, -ēre, correspondī, correspōnsum: to correspond
culpa, -ae f.: faul, guilt
ēmittō, -ere, ēmīsī, ēmissum: to let go
filius, -ī m.: son
inclīnō (1): to lower
Īsidōrus, -ī m.: Isidore (of Seville)
lignum, -ī n.: wood; tree
passiō, -ōnis f.: suffering
peragō, -ere, perēgī, perāctum: to execute, complete

pōmum, -ī n.: fruit
ratiō, -ōnis f.: reason
sacrāmentum, -ī n.: sacrament
satisfaciō, -facere, -fēcī, -factum: to make amends
spīritus, -ūs m.: life, spirit
testor, testārī, testātus sum: to bear witness
trīnitās, -tātis f.: the Trinity
unde: from which place, for this reason
ūnigenitus, -a, -um: only-begotten
vetō, vetāre, vetuī, vetitum: to forbid

Īsidōrus: Nogorola attributes this quotation to Isidore of Seville, the seventh-century author of the *Etymologiae*; however, it is in fact Hilary of Poitiers (a fourth-century bishop) as quoted by Thomas Aquinas (*Summa Theologica* Book III q.46 a.5.1)

ad peragendum...sacrāmentum: *to complete the sacrament; ad* + gerundive phrase to express purpose

cōnsummāsse...testātur: *testātur* sets up an indirect statement: *sē cōnsummā(vi)sse omne genus passiōnum*

Ratiō: *the reason (being);* Christ's punishment (*poena*) had to be proportional to Adam's sin (*culpa*)

Augustīnus: "Contempsit Ādam praeceptum" (et nōn dīxit "Ēva") "accipiēns ex arbore pōmum, sed quidquid Ādam perdidit, Chrīstus invēnit." Psalmō LXVIII.°: "Quae nōn rapuī tunc exsolvēbam." Ergō peccātum Ādae fuit maximum, quia poena correspondēns culpae fuit maxima et fuit generālis hominibus. Apostolus: "Omnēs peccāvērunt in Ādam."

---

apostolus, -ī m.: apostle

arbor, -oris f.: tree

Augustīnus, -ī m.: Augustine

Chrīstus, -ī m.: Christ

contemnō, -ere, contempsī, contemptum: to pay no heed

correspondeō, -ēre, correspondī, correspōnsum: to correspond

culpa, -ae f.: guilt

exsolvō, -ere, exsolvī, exsolūtum: to resolve, pay off

generālis, -e: general, shared by or common to a kind

inveniō, -īre, invēnī, inventum: to find

maximus, -a, -um: greatest

perdō, -ere, perdidī, perditum: to lose, ruin

pōmum, -ī n.: fruit

praeceptum, -ī n.: command

psalmus, -ī m.: psalm

rapiō, -ere, rapuī, raptum: to take, seize

"Contempsit Ādam...Chrīstus invēnit": Nogarola takes this quotation from Thomas Aquinas *Summa Theologica* (III q.46 a.4); Aquinas wrongly attributed it to Augustine, and it is in fact Julius Firmicus Maternus *Dē Errōre Profānārum Religiōnum* 26 (*PL* 12.1038)

(et nōn dīxit "Ēva"): *and he does not say "Eve"*; Nogorola interjects into the quotation to highlight her point; the subject here is Augustine, not Adam

Psalmō LXVIII.°: Psalm 69:4 in modern Bibles; in the Clementine Vulgate it is numbered as 68:5

"Quae nōn rapuī tunc exsolvēbam": *I paid for what I did not steal*

Apostolus: *the Apostle (Paul)*; a paraphrase of Romans 5:12

Omnēs...Ādam: *All sinned in Adam*; Adam's sin transferred to the rest of humanity

4.9 "Omnis etiam Ādae culpa Ēvae ascrībitur, quia teste Aristotīle 'quidquid est causa causae est causa causātī.'" Haec vēra sunt in iīs quae sunt, ut melius nōstī, aliōrum per sē causae, quod pār est dē causā prīmā, prīncipiō prīmō, et "propter quod ūnum quodque tāle." Quod nōn vidēs in Ēvā fuisse, quia Ādam vel līberum habuit arbitrium, vel nōn; sī nōn habuit, nūllum peccātum habuit;

---

arbitrium, -ī n.: will, choice
Aristotīlēs, -is m.: Aristotle
ascrībō, -ere, ascrīpsī, ascrīptum: to ascribe, attribute
causō (1): to cause
culpa, -ae f.: guilt
melius: better, very well (comp. adv.)

nōscō, -ere, nōvī, nōtum: to learn; know (in perfect tenses)
pār, paris: equal; right, fit
prīncipium, -ī n.: beginning, foundation
propter (+ acc): on account of
testis, -is m.: witness
vērus, -a, -um: true

"Omnis etiam…causātī": Nogarola quotes Foscarini's statement from 3.9
teste Aristotīle: *with Aristotle as our witness;* abl. absolute; as noted in the commentary on 3.9 above, the quotation is from the pseudo-Aristotelian *Liber Dē Causīs*, as quoted by Duns Scotus *Quaestiōnēs Subtilissimae in Metaphysicam* V q.1
'quidquid…causātī': *whatever is the cause (quidquid est causa) of a cause (causae) is the cause (est causa) of the thing caused (causātī);* Foscarini argued that Eve was responsible for Adam's sin
Haec vēra sunt in iīs quae sunt…causae: *These (words) are true in those (things) which are…causes;* Nogarola will argue that this is not true in Eve's case
ut melius nōstī: *as you know very well;* the *nōstī* = *nōvistī*, meaning "learn" in the present tense and meaning "know" in the perfect tense
aliōrum per sē causae: *causes of other things by means of themselves;* things that directly cause other things to happen without any other external factors
quod pār est: *which is right;* idiom
"propter quod ūnum quodque tāle": *on account of which thing each thing (is) such (as it is);* on this scholastic phrase, see the commentary on 3.9
Quod nōn vidēs: *Which you do not see;* the *quod* here is referring to something that is a cause with no other factors (*per sē*)

77

sī habuit, ergō Ēva coēgit illud quod fierī nōn potest. Nam Bernardus: "Līberum arbitrium [207] prō ingenitā nōbilitāte ā nūllā cōgitur necessitāte, neque ā Deō, quia sī sīc, esset dare duo opposita stāre simul." Nōn potest igitur Deus facere quod aliqua operātiō ā līberō prōcēdat arbitriō ipsō manente, et nōn līberē sed coāctē fiat. Augustīnus super Genesī:

arbitrium, -ī n.: will, choice
Augustīnus, -ī m.: Augustine
Bernardus, -ī m.: Bernard (of Clairvaux, 11th-12th century)
coāctē: under compulsion (adv.)
Genesis, -is f.: (Book of) Genesis
igitur: therefore
maneō, -ēre, mānsī, mānsum: to remain

necessitās, -tātis f.: necessity
nōbilitās, -tātis f.: nobility
operātiō, -ōnis f.: action
opposita, -ōrum n.: opposites, contrary propositions
prōcēdō, -ere, -cessī, -cessum: to proceed
simul: at same time
super (+ abl): over, concerning

Ēva...illud: *Eve compelled that which cannot happen;* illud refers to Eve compelling Adam's actions despite his free will
Bernardus: *Bernard;* this quotation reflects ideas from Bernard's *On Grace and Free Choice* 1.2 and 4.9 (*PL* 182:1002, 1006–7), but seems to be taken from Thomas Aquinas (*Dē Vēritāte* q.22 a.5) or Thomas of Argentina (*Comm. Sent.* 2 d.25 a.3)
neque ā Deō: *not even by God*
sī sīc (esset): *if that were the case*
esset...simul: *it would be to grant two contrary propositions to stand at the same time;* not even God can force free will, because then it would not truly be free
facere quod...operātiō...prōcēdat: *to make...an action...proceed;* an indirect command starting with *quod* rather than *ut*
ipsō manente: *with it (free will) still remaining itself;* abl. absolute
Augustīnus super Genesī: *Augustine concerning Genesis;* similar ideas are expressed in *Dē Genesī ad Litteram* 11.9–16 (*PL* 34:434–58), but versions of this idea appear in various scholastic sources

"Nōn potest Deus facere contrā nātūram quam bonā voluntāte īnstituit."

4.10 Posset autem Deus ipse auferre illam lībertātis conditiōnem ad utrumlibet et dare aliam, sīcut nōn potest ignis, ignis manēns, nōn combūrere nisi tālis nātūra mūtētur et ad tempus suspendātur virtūte dīvīnā. Ergō minus alia creātūra ā Deō, ut angelus bonus vel diabolus;

angelus, -ī m.: angel
auferō, auferre, abstulī, ablātum: to remove
combūrō, -ere, combūssī, combūstum: to burn
conditiō, -ōnis f.: condition, situation
contrā (+ acc): against
creātūra, -ae f.: creation; creature
creō (1): to create
diabolus, -ī m.: devil
dīvīnus, -a, -um: divine
īnstituō, -ere, īnstituī, īnstitūtum: to establish, build

lībertās, -tātis f.: freedom, liberty
maneō, -ēre, mānsī, mānsum: to remain
minus: less (adv.)
mūtō (1): to alter, change
sīcut: just like, in the same way
suspendō, -ere, suspendī, suspēnsum: to suspend
uterlibet, -tralibet, -trumlibet: whichever/whatever one pleases
voluntās, -tātis f.: will, purpose

facere contrā nātūram: *to act contrary to nature*
ad utrumlibet: *for any reason at all;* an idiom of scholastic Latin
aliam (conditiōnem): *another (condition);* that is, God could grant a state other than free will
ignis manēns: *while remaining fire*
ad tempus: an idiom meaning "for some time"
virtūte: *power;* a common meaning for *virtūs* in post-classical Latin
minus alia creātūra ā Deō (possit): *therefore another creature than God (would be able to) less*
ut angelus bonus vel diabolus: *like a good angel or the devil*

multō minus fēmina, quae imperfectior et dēbilior est iīs. Et assignat Augustīnus ratiōnem dīcēns: "Suprā [208] mentem nostram nihil praeter Deum, nec inter Deum et mentem nostram est aliquid medium." Cōgēns autem oportet quod sit suprā id quod cōgitur; sed Ēva fuit īnferior Ādam, ergō nōn fuit ipsa causa peccātī. Ecclēsiasticī XV.°:

assīgnō (1): to assign; attribute

Augustīnus, -ī m.: Augustine

dēbilis, -e: weak

fēmina, -ae f.: woman

imperfectus, -a, -um: imperfect

īnferior, īnferius: inferior, lower (comp. adj.)

medius, -a, -um: intermediate

mēns, -ntis f.: mind

minus: less (adv.)

multō: by much, a great deal (adv.)

oportet, oportēre, oportuit: it is necessary, it is proper

praeter (+ acc): besides, except

ratiō, -ōnis f.: reason, rationale

suprā (+ acc): above

iīs: *than them;* abl. of comparison referring to the *angelus* and *diabolus*

Augustīnus: Nogarola takes the quotation from Thomas Aquinas (*Scrīptum Super Sententiīs* Book II d.23 q.2 art.1), who attributes it to Augustine, possibly referring to *Dē Vērā Religiōne* 113 (*PL* 34.172) or *Dē Dīversīs Quaestiōnibus* 51.4 (*PL* 40.33)

nihil (est) praeter Deum: *(there is) nothing except God*

Cōgēns…cōgitur: The thing compelling (*cōgēns*) must be (*oportet*) a thing which (*quod*) is superior to (*suprā*) that which (*id quod*) is compelled (*cōgitur*); Eve could not have compelled Adam to sin because she is not superior to him

īnferior Ādam: *īnferior to Adam;* literally, "lower than Adam"; abl. of comparison, but the word *Ādam* is only declined in the genitive

Ecclēsiasticī XV.°: Sirach, 15:14–15; the Hebrew Book of Sirach is called Ecclesiasticus in the Latin Vulgate; Nogarola here paraphrases

"Deus ab initiō cōnstituit hominem et relīquit eum in manū cōnsiliī suī adiēcitque mandāta et praecepta sua. Sī volueris mandāta servāre, cōnservābunt tē et fidem placitam facient." Unde Ādam accūsāre Deum potius vīsus est quam sē excūsāre, cum dīxit: "Socia quam dedistī mihi fēcit mē peccāre."

4.11 Quod autem facilius potuerit amīcissima socia virum dēcipere, quam turpissimus serpēns mulierem,

---

accūsō (1): to accuse, blame

cōnservō (1): to preserve, protect, keep

cōnstituō, -ere, cōnstituī, cōnstitūtum: to set up, make

dēcipiō, -ere, dēcēpī, dēceptum: to deceive

excūsō (1): to excuse

facilius: more easily (comp. adv.)

initium, -ī n.: the beginning

mandātum, -ī n.: command, commandment

placeō, -ēre, placuī, placitum: to please

potius: rather

praeceptum, -ī n.: command

serpēns, -ntis m.: serpent, snake

servō (1): to preserve, protect, keep

socia, -ae f.: partner

turpis, -e: nasty; disgraceful

unde: from which, for which reason

---

in manū cōnsiliī suī: *in the hands of (man's) own judgment;* that is, God made humans and gave them free will, leaving them in the hands of their own judgment

Sī volueris mandāta servāre: *if you voluntarily keep the commandments;* the verb *velle* can have a sense of "to do (something) voluntarily"

fidem placitam facient: *they will make faith your free choice;* literally, "make faith a thing decided (by you)"; *placitus* (the perfect passive of *placēre*) can have the sense of "having been decided"

Ādam...vīsus est: *Adam seemed;* perfect passive of *vidēre*

"Socia...fēcit mē peccāre": *the companion...made me sin;* Gen. 3:12; the predicate *mē peccāre* is acting as an objective noun clause (= CL *fēcit ut peccārem*)

Quod autem...potuerit: *As to the fact that she might have been able;* noun clause with a subjunctive of reported reason, recalling Foscarini's argument in 3.11

quam...serpēns mulierem: *than the serpent (deceive) the woman;* the verb is carried over from the previous clause

multō minus peccāvit Ēva dēbilis et ignōrāns secundum nātūram, dīcō, [209] astūtissimō illī serpentī assentiendō, quī interpretātus est sapiēns, quam Ādam ā Deō in perfectā scientiā et cognitiōne creātus persuāsiōnem et vōcem imperfectae mulieris audiendō.

4.12 Quod autem longius Ēva persevērāverit, ergō magis peccāverit,

---

assentior, assentīrī, assēnsus sum (+ dat.): to assent to; agree with

astūtus, -a, -um: clever, cunning

cognitiō, -ōnis f.: capacity to learn, understanding

creō (1): to create

dēbilis, -e: weak

ignōrāns, -ntis: ignorant

imperfectus, -a, -um: imperfect, incomplete

interpretor, interpretārī, interpretātus sum: to explain; understand

longē: for a long while (adv.)

minus: less (adv.)

multō: by much, a great deal (adv.)

perfectus, -a, -um: perfect, complete

persevērō (1): to persist; continue

persuāsiō, -ōnis f.: persuasion

sapiēns, sapientis: wise

scientia, -ae f.: knowledge

secundum (+ acc.): in accordance with

serpēns, -ntis m.: serpent, snake

---

multō minus peccāvit Ēva...assentiendō...quam Ādam...audiendō: *Eve sinned much less...by assenting...than Adam by listening;* the *assentiendō* and *audiendō* are gerunds in the abl. of means, functioning with Eve and Adam respectively

peccāvit...dīcō: *Eve sinned, I say;* the *dīcō* is a parenthetical insertion

quī interpretātus est: *who has been understood as wise; interpretor* here is being used with a passive meaning, despite being a deponent verb

in...cognitiōne: *in (a state of) perfect knowledge and understanding;* metaphorical use of *in* to refer to states, rather than locations

Quod...persevērāverit...peccāverit: *As to the fact that;* noun clause with subjunctives of reported reason, referring back to Foscarini's argument in 3.12

quia tantō graviōra sunt dēlicta quantō diūtius īnfēlīcem animam tenent alligātam, scīlicet vērum est, cum peccāta sint pariā et in eōdem vel in similī. Sed Ādam et Ēva nōn fuērunt parēs, quia Ādam animal perfectum et Ēva imperfectum et ignōrāns.

4.13 Tandem, ut tē auctōre ūtar: "Mulier exemplum et causa peccātī fuit, et in exemplum vehementer Gregōrius culpam extendit,

alligō (1): to bind

anima, -ae f.: soul

animal, animālis n.: animal, creature

auctor, auctōris m.: authority

culpa, -ae f.: blame

dēlictum, -ī n.: offense, crime; sin

diū: (for) a long time

exemplum, -ī n.: example; precedent

extendō, -ere, extendī, extēnsum: to stretch; extend

Gregōrius, -ī m.: Gregory (the Great)

ignōrāns, -ntis: ignorant

imperfectus, -a, -um: imperfect, incomplete

īnfēlīx, īnfēlīcis: wretched, unlucky

pār, paris: equal

perfectus, -a, -um: perfect, complete

quantō: by how much, the more

scīlicet: certainly; of course

similis, -e: similar

tandem: finally

tantō: so much (adv.)

ūtor, ūtī, ūsus sum (+ abl.): to use

vehementer: ardently

vērus, -a, -um: true

dēlicta...alligātam: *by how much longer the sins hold the unfortunate soul in bondage;* the longer a person has been in a sinful state, the more serious the offense should be considered to be; this is still Foscarini's argument from 3.12

in eōdem vel in similī (homine): *in the same person or a similar one; eōdem* and *similī* are acting substantively

Ādam (est) animal perfectum: the verb "to be" is implicit

Ēva (est animal) imperfectum et ignōrāns: adjectives are neuter with an assumed *animal*

Tandem, ut tē auctōre ūtar: *finally, so that I may use you as my authority;* essentially "if I may quote you"; Nogarola here is quoting from 3.13

in exemplum...culpam extendit: *he extends guilt to the example;* the idea is from Gregory's *Liber Rēgulae Pastōrālis* 1.2 (*PL* 77.15–16)

et causam ignōrantium Iūdaeōrum, quia prīma fuit, magis damnāvit Chrīstus [210] quam sententiam Pīlātī doctiōris, cum dīxit: 'Proptereā quī mē tibi trādidit maius peccātum habet.'" Dīcō quod Chrīstus causam ignōrantium Iūdaeōrum nōn damnāvit quia prīma fuerit, sed quia erat ex propriā malitiā atque obstinātiōne prāvā et diabolicā.

Chrīstus, -ī m.: (Jesus) Christ
damnō (1): condemn
diabolicus, -a, -um: devilish
doctus, -a, -um: learned, wise
ignōrāns, -ntis: ignorant
Iūdaeus, -ī m.: Judean; Jewish person; the Jews (pl.)
maior, maius: greater (comp. adj.)
malitia, -ae f.: malice
obstinātiō, -ōnis f.: determination, stubbornness

Pīlātus, -ī m.: Pontius Pilate (prefect of Judaea, 26-36 CE)
prāvus, -a, -um: vicious
proprius, -a, -um: particular, characteristic
proptereā: therefore, for this reason
sententia, -ae f.: opinion; sentence (legal)
trādō, -ere, trādidī, trāditum: to hand over; deliver

---

causam...damnāvit...quam senteniam: *condemned the case of the ignorant Jews more than learned Pilate's sentence;* both *causam* and *sententiam* are objects of *damnāvit*

ignōrantium Iūdaeōrum: *of the ignorant Jews;* an antisemitic epithet; for more on antisemitism in the *Defense of Eve*, see Introduction IV

Pīlātī doctiōris: *of the quite learned Pilate;* Pontius Pilate was the Roman prefect of Judaea who ordered the crucifixion of Jesus

Dīcō quod...damnāvit: *I say that Christ...condemned;* post-classical use of *quod* + indicative for indirect statement; Nogarola uses the *dīcō* here to mark the beginning of her response to Foscarini's argument recounted in the previous sentence

ex propriā malitiā: *from their special malice;* another antisemitic argument; see Introduction IV

Nōn enim ex ignōrantiā peccābant, quia magis ignōrāns dē hīs erat Pīlātus gentīlis, quam Iūdaeī, quī Lēgem et prophētās habēbant et legēbant, et dē eō quotīdiē signa vidēbant. Nam Iōannis XV.°: "Sī nōn vēnissem et locūtus eīs nōn fuissem, peccātum nōn habērent, nunc autem excūsātiōnem nōn habent dē peccātō suō."

excūsātiō, -ōnis f.: excuse
gentīlis, -e: gentile, non-Jew
ignōrāns, -ntis: ignorant
ignōrantia, -ae f.: ignorance
Iōannēs, -is m.: John (apostle)
Iūdaeus, -ī m.: Judean, Jewish person; the Jews (pl.)
legō, -ere, lēgī, lēctum: to read

lēx, lēgis f.: law; the Law (of Moses)
loquor, loquī, locūtus sum: to speak
Pīlātus, -ī m.: Pontius Pilate (prefect of Judaea, 26-36 CE)
prophēta, -ae m.: prophet
quotīdiē: every day
signum, -ī n.: indication; sign

magis ignōrāns...erat Pīlātus gentīlis: *Pilate the gentile was more ignorant;* the subject here is *Pīlātus*, the predicate *ignōrāns*

dē hīs: *concerning these matters;* "matters" refers to Jesus' status as the Messiah; Nogarola argues that since Pilate did not know the Hebrew Bible, he would not have been able to understand the same signs of the Messiah that the Judeans (according to Nogarola) should have been able to

Lēgem...habēbant et legēbant: *they had and read the Law and the prophets;* imperfect with habitual aspect; Nogarola assumes that the writings of the Hebrew Bible would have made Jesus's status as the Messiah obvious and undeniable

dē eō...signa: *signs concerning it;* the *eō* is the divinity of Jesus, and *signa* the miraculous signs that would have indicated that status

"Sī nōn...habērent": *If I had not come... then they would not (now) have;* John 15:22; mixed contrafactual condition, the if-clause is in the pluperfect subjunctive (*vēnissem, locūtus fuissem*), the then-clause is in the imperfect subjunctive (*habērent*)

Unde ipsī dīxērunt: "Quid facimus, quia hic homō multa signa facit?" Item: "Dīc nōbīs palam sī tū es Chrīstus!" Nam populus iste pecūliāris erat Deō et ipse Chrīstus: "Nōn sum missus nisi ad ovēs Isrāēl, [211] quae perierant ... Nōn est bonum sūmere pānem dē manibus filiōrum et dare canibus." Ergō magis peccāvērunt Iūdaeī, quia plūs eōs Iēsūs dīligēbat.

canis, canis m.: dog
Chrīstus, -ī m.: (Jesus) Christ
dīligō, -ere, dīlēxī, dīlēctum: to value, love
filius, filiī m.: son
Iēsus, Iēsū m.: Jesus
Isrāēl m.: Israel (undeclined)
item: likewise; also
Iūdaeus, -ī m.: Jew, Jewish person; the Jews (pl.)
mittō, -ere, mīsī, missum: to send
ovis, ovis f.: sheep

palam: plainly
pānis, pānis m.: bread
pecūliāris, -e: special; singular, exceptional
pereō, -īre, perīvī (-iī), peritum: to be lost
plūs: more (adv.)
signum, -ī n.: indication; sign
sūmō, -ere, sūmpsī, sūmptum: to take
unde: from where, for which reason, that's why

ipsī (Iūdaeī) dīxērunt: *they themselves (the Judeans) said;* it is the priests and Pharisees specifically who say the following quotation; another instance of Nogarola's antisemitism, extending the words of the Pharisees and Priests to the entirety of the Jewish people

"Quid facimus...facit": *"What do we do?";* John 11:47; present with a future sense

"Dīc nōbīs...Chrīstus": *"Tell us plainly if you are Christ!";* paraphrased from John 10:24

"Nōn sum missus nisi...": *I was only sent to;* from Matthew 15:24; literally, "I was not sent except to" (perfect passive indicative)

ovēs Isrāēl: *the sheep of Israel;* that is, the Israelites

"Nōn est bonum...canibus": from Matthew 15:26; the "sons" in this metaphor are the Jewish people, and the "dogs" are the gentiles

4.14 Et haec ā mē fēminā inermī et pauperculā dicta sufficiant.

5.1 Rēspōnsiō Lodovīcī et Conclūsiō Quaestiōnis: Ita omnia dīvīnissimē complexa es, ut nēdum ex philosophantium et theologōrum fontibus, sed ex caelō tua scrīpta collāpsa crēdere possīmus. Idcircō ea potius laude quam contrādictiōne digna sunt.

---

collābor, collābī, collāpsum sum: to collapse, fall down
complector, complectī, complexus sum: to encircle, encompass
conclūsiō, -ōnis f.: conclusion
contrādictiō, -ōnis f.: objection
dictum, -ī n.: word
dignus, -a, -um (+ abl.): meriting
dīvīnus, -a, -um: divine
fēmina, -ae f.: woman
fōns, fontis m.: fount; source
idcircō: on that account; therefore
inermis, -e: unarmed

laus, laudis f.: praise
nēdum: still less; not just … but even (with sed)
pauperculus, -a, -um: poor
philosophāns, -ntis m.: philosopher
potius: rather
quaestiō, -ōnis f.: question, inquiry
rēspōnsiō, -ōnis f.: response
scrīptum, -ī n.: a written work
sufficiō, -ere, suffēcī, suffectum: to be sufficient
theologus, -ī m.: theologian

---

haec ā mē fēminā…dicta: *these words said by me, a poor and unarmed woman; haec* and *dicta* bracket the qualifying phrase *ā mē fēminā inermī et pauperculā*
nēdum…fontibus, sed ex caelō: *not just from the founts…but even from heaven;* take closely with *collapse* ("have fallen")
scrīpta collāpsa (esse) crēdere possīmus: *I could believe that (your) writings have fallen;* *crēdere* sets up an indirect statement: *scrīpta collāpsa (esse)*
ea (scrīpta): *these (writings)*

Nē tamen coeptā ūtilitāte fraudēris, accipe quae brevissimē in dīversam sententiam dīcī possunt, ut melliflua paradīsī sēmina iactēs, quae legentēs dēlectent et tē glōriā illūstrent.

5.2 Ignōrantia Ēvae crassissima fuit, quia māluit daemonī quam creātōrī fidem praestāre. Quae quidem ignōrantia ex eius dēlictō (ut sacra testātur historia) prōcessit, ideō peccātum [212] nōn excūsat.

---

brevis, -e: short, concise

coepī, coepisse, coeptum: to begin

crassus, -a, -um: thick, deep; crass

creātor, -ōris m.: creator

daemōn, -onis m.: demon

dēlectō (1): to delight, please

dēlictum, -ī n.: fault

dīversus, -a, -um: opposite; different

excūsō (1): to excuse, justify

fraudō (1): to steal; cheat

glōria, -ae f.: glory

historia, -ae f.: history

iactō (1): to throw, scatter, sow

ideō: therefore

ignōrantia, -ae f.: ignorance

illūstrō (1): to illuminate

legō, -ere, lēgī, lēctum: to read

mālō, mālle, māluī: to prefer

mellifluus, -a, -um: flowing with honey

paradīsus, -ī m.: paradise

praestō, -āre, praestitī, praestitum: to furnish, supply

prōcēdō, -ere, prōcessī, prōcessum: to proceed

sacer, -cra, -crum: sacred, holy

sēmen, sēminis n.: seed

sententia, -ae f.: opinion; thought

testor, testārī, testātus sum: to attest

ūtilitās, -tātis f.: usefulness

Nē...coeptā ūtilitāte fraudēris: *Lest you be cheated of the utility (of what we have) begun;* literally, "of the having-been-begun utility"

ut melliflua paradīsī sēmina iactēs: *so you might sow the sweet seeds of paradise;* purpose clause; a reference to the idea of having Nogarola disseminate their work

quae...dēlectent...illūstrent: *which may* (or: *in order to*) *delight readers and illuminate you with glory;* relative clause, which could be purpose or characteristic

legentēs: *readers;* literally "those reading (this work)"

Ignōrantia Ēvae crassissima...quia māluit daemonī...prastāre: *The ignorance of Eve was most crass...because she preferred to put her faith in the demon;* a reference to 4.2, where Nogarola argues that the ignorant sin less if they put their faith in God

Quae quidem ignōrantia: *And indeed this ignorance;* a connecting relative

Immō, sī vērum fatērī licet, extrēma dēmentia fuit nōn manēre in terminīs quōs Deus optimus sibi cōnstituerat, vānāque spē ducta caruit habitīs et ambītīs.

5.3 Et nē illa dīvidam quae tū prūdentissimē coniūnxistī: incōnstantia Ēvae damnāta mōris fuit et nōn nātūrae; quia in iīs quae ā nātūrā īnsunt, nec laudāmur nec vituperāmur sapientissimōrum philosophantium iūdiciō.

ambiō, -īre, ambīvī, ambītum: to go round; to strive for

careō, -ēre, caruī, caritum (+ abl.): to be without; lack

coniungō, -ere, coniūnxī, coniūnctum: to join together

cōnstituō, -ere, cōnstituī, cōnstitūtum: to set up

damnō (1): to condemn

dēmentia, -ae f.: insanity

dīvidō, -ere, dīvīsī, dīvīsum: to divide

dūcō, -ere, dūxī, ductum: to lead

extrēmus, -a, -um: most extreme

fateor, fatērī, fassus sum: to admit

immō: on the contrary; indeed

incōnstantia, -ae f.: inconstancy

īnsum, inesse, īnfuī: to be in; belong to

iūdicium, -ī n.: judgment

laudō (1): to praise, approve

maneō, -ēre, mānsī, mānsum: to stay

philosophāns, -ntis m.: philosopher

prūdenter: wisely; prudently

sapiēns, sapientis: rational; wise

terminus, -ī m.: boundary, limit

vānus, -a, -um: empty, vain

vērum, -ī n.: the truth

vituperō (1): to blame

vānāque spē ducta: *lead by vain hope;* the *ducta* here is the nom. of the perf. pass. participle of *dūcere*, agreeing with an assumed "Eve"

caruit habitīs et ambītīs: *she lost what she had and what she wanted;* habitīs and ambītīs are perf. pass. participles acting as substantives, literally "what was had (by her)" and "what was reached for (by her)"

Et nē illa dīvidam: *And lest I divide those (things) which you so wisely joined;* Nogarola joins ignorance and inconstancy in 4.2–4.3

incōnstantia Ēvae damnāta…fuit: *Eve's inconstancy was condemned;* = CL *damnāta est*

mōris…nōn nātūrae: *for (its) character, not (its) nature;* gen. of charge with *damnāta fuit*

Optima fuit etiam mulieris nātūra et ratiōnī, generī, temporī oboediēns, quoniam velutī ferīs dentēs, armentīs cornua, volucribus pennae datae sunt ad vītam, ita mulierī ratiō ad retinendam et cōnsequendam animae salūtem sufficiēns.

5.4 Sī ad virī adiūtōrium, perfectiōnem, sōlātium et gaudium Ēva nātūrāliter creāta fuit, contrā nātūrae lēgēs sē gessit virō labōrēs,

---

adiūtōrium, -ī n.: assistance
anima, -ae f.: soul
armentum, -ī n.: cattle, herd
cōnsequor, cōnsequī, cōnsecūtus sum: to follow after; attain
contrā (+ acc.): against, contrary to
cornū, -ūs n.: horn
creō (1): to create
dēns, dentis m.: tooth; tusk
ferus, -ī m.: wild beast, animal
gaudium, -ī n.: joy
labōrō (1): to work; suffer
legō, -ere, lēgī, lēctum: to read
lēx, lēgis f.: law

nātūrāliter: naturally
oboediēns, -entis (+ dat.): obedient
optimus, -a, -um: best
penna, -ae f.: feather, wing
perfectiō, -ōnis f.: perfection
quoniam: since, because
ratiō, -ōnis f.: rationality; reason
retineō, -ēre, retinuī, retentum: to retain
salūs, salūtis f.: health; salvation
sōlātium, -ī n.: comfort
sufficiēns, -entis: sufficient
velutī: just as
volucer, volucris: bird

---

ratiōnī, generī, temporī oboediēns: *obeying reason, sex, and age;* literally "obedient to reason, type, time"

ita mulierī ratiō (data est): *so to the woman reason was given;* the verb must be supplied from the previous clause

ad...adiūtōrium, perfectiōnem, sōlātium et gaudium: *to assist, perfect, comfort, and gladden;* literally "for the assistance, perfection, comfort, and joy"; the *ad* here carries a sense of purpose; *sōlātium* is an alternate spelling for *sōlācium*

creāta fuit: = CL *creāta est*

sē gessit: *she behaved;* literally, "she carried herself"

imperfectiōnēs, trīstitiās et moerōrēs subministrandō, quae scelera gravissima fore sacra [213] dēcrēta sānxērunt. Nec hūmānae lēgēs, diūtissimē clārissimōrum virōrum ingeniīs dīgestae, sine certā ratiōne īnstituērunt quod aliēnae reī contractātiō quantō magis fit contrā dominī voluntātem, tantō graviōrem poenam merētur.

aliēnus, -a, -um: another's

certus, -a, -um: certain

clārus, -a, -um: clear; famous

contrā (+ acc.): against

contractātiō, -ōnis f.: taking, seizure

dēcrētum, -ī n.: doctrine

dīgerō, -ere, dīgessī, dīgestum: to arrange

diū: (for) a long time

hūmānus, -a, -um: human

imperfectiō, -ōnis f.: imperfection

ingenium, -ī n.: talent, genius

īnstituō, -ere, īnstituī, īnstitūtum: to establish

lēx, lēgis f.: law

mereor, merērī, meritus sum: to earn, merit

moeror, -ōris m.: grief

quantō: by how much (adv.)

ratiō, -ōnis f.: reason

sacer, sacra, sacrum: holy

sanciō, -īre, sānxī, sānctum: to confirm

subministrō (1): to supply

tantō: (by) so much (adv.)

trīstitia, -ae f.: sadness

voluntās, -tātis f.: will, desire

subministrandō: *by supplying;* gerund in abl. of means; literally "by supplying X, Y, and Z to her husband"

fore: *would be;* fut. inf. (= *futūrum esse*) in an indirect statement set up by *sānxērunt*

sacra dēcrēta: *holy doctrines;* subject of *sānxērunt*

Nec hūmānae lēgēs...sine certā ratiōne īnstituērunt: *Nor have human laws...established without certain reason;* double negative

dīgestae: nom. participle agreeing with *lēgēs*

quod: the start of an indirect statement following *īnstituērunt*

aliēnae reī contractātiō: *the taking of another's property;* a paraphrase of Roman law (*Dīgesta* 47.2.1§3; cf. *Institutes* 4.1.1), as formulated by Azo of Bologna (*Summa Codicis* 6.1 no.1); *contractātiō* is an alternate spelling for *contrectātiō*

quantō...tantō: *by however much...by that much;* the more it happens contrary to the owner's will, the greater punishment is due to the perpetrator

5.5 Quod scrībīs dē mandātōrum trānsgressiōne Ēvam nōn līberat, quae nec ipsa servāvit.

5.6 In quō autem differant peccātum angelī et hominis, lātissimus campus est et velutī tuō clārissimō ingeniō dignissimus cibus, ita hāc temporis angustiā longē amplior.

amplus, -a, -um: spacious
angelus, -ī m.: angel
angustia, -ae f.: narrow space
campus, -ī m.: plain; field
cibus, -ī m.: food
clārus, -a, -um: clear, brilliant
differō, differre, distulī, dīlātum: to differ
dignus, -a, -um (+ abl.): worthy
ingenium, -ī n.: talent, mind

lātus, -a, -um: wide
līberō (1): to free; acquit
longē: long, far (adv.)
mandātum, -ī n.: command
minus: less (adv.)
scrībō, -ere, scrīpsī, scrīptum: to write
servō (1): to preserve, save
trānsgressiō, -ōnis f.: transgression
velutī: just as

Quod scrībīs: *That which you write;* rel. clause, the implicit antecedent (*id*) is subject the of *līberat*

quae nec ipsa servāvit: *which not even she herself preserved;* the antecedent of *quae* is *mandātōrum*; that is, Eve also transgressed God's commands

differant peccātum angelī et hominis: *the sin of angel and man differ;* although *peccātum* is singular but functions as a plural (the sin of angel and the sin of man)

hāc temporis angustiā longē amplior: *far too vast (a topic) for this narrow span of time;* literally "far larger than this narrow span of time"; abl. of comparison

5.7 Quōmodo autem ratiōnī bonitātis summī Deī convenīre sentiās maiōra mala illīs quī minus peccāvēre diffundere, nōn bene concipiō.

5.8 Nimium stringis Aristotīlis testimōnia ad prīmās causās, nam omnis causa causae est causa causātī.

5.9 Et quia līberī arbitriī fuit Ādam, nōn faciō ipsum dēlictī inmūnem, et licet omnis Ādae culpa quādam ex parte Ēvae per mē ascrīpta sit, nōn tamen omnis et omnimoda causa Ēvae fuit.

---

arbitrium, -ī n.: choice, judgment
Aristotīlēs, -is m.: Aristotle
ascrībō, -ere, ascrīpsī, ascrīptum: to ascribe
bonitās, -tātis f.: goodness
causō (1): to cause
concipiō, -ere, concēpī, conceptum: to conceive, understand
conveniō, -īre, convēnī, conventum (+ dat.): to be compatible with, fit
culpa, -ae f.: fault
dēlictum, -ī n.: sin, fault
diffundō, -ere, diffūndī, diffūsum: to pour out

inmūnis, -e (+ gen.): free from
licet (+ subj.): although
maior, maius: greater (adj.)
nimium: too much (adv.)
omnimodus, -a, -um: of every sort
quōmodo: how
ratiō, -ōnis f.: plan, reasoning
sentiō, -īre, sēnsī, sēnsum: to perceive; think
stringō, -ere, strīnxī, strictum: to draw tight; squeeze
summus, -a, -um: highest
testimōnium, -ī n.: testimony

Quōmodo…sentiās: *How you think;* indirect question set up by *concipiō*
peccāvēre: = *peccāvērunt*
Aristotīlis testimōnia ad prīmās causās: *Aristotle's testimonies on first causes;* see Nogarola's argument at 4.9
līberī arbitriī fuit Ādam: *Adam was a man of free will;* gen. of characteristic
nōn faciō: *I do not consider;* literally "I do not make him to be free from guilt"
quādam ex parte: *to some extent;* literally, "from a certain part"
nōn tamen omnis et omnimoda causa Ēvae fuit: *was not entirely and in every way a cause of Eve;* the implied subject is *Ādae culpa*

Dē līberō arbitriō [214]et bonitāte nātūrae nōn contrādīcō.

5.10 Dē facilitāte cōnsēnsūs virī dictīs mulieris, volō sexūs illīus dēceptiōnēs ad tē scrībēns silentiō praeterīre, sed hōc vetustissimō verbō mea firmētur ratiō: "Nūlla pestis efficācior est ad nocendum quam familiāris inimīcus."

5.11 Magnum prīma māter excitāvit incendium,

arbitrium, -ī n.: choice, judgment
bonitās, -ātis f.: goodness
cōnsēnsus, -ūs m.: agreement
contrādīcō, -ere, contrādīxī, contrādictum: to contradict, speak against
dēceptiō, -ōnis f.: deceitfulness
dictum, -ī n.: word
efficāx, efficācis: effective
excitō (1): to stir up, kindle
facilitās, -tātis f.: facility, ease
familiāris, -e: intimate, friendly

firmō (1): to strengthen, confirm
incendium, -ī n.: fire, conflagration
inimīcus, -ī m.: enemy
noceō, -ēre, nocuī, nocitum: to harm
pestis, -is f.: plague
praetereō, -īre, praeterīvī, praeteritum: to pass by
ratiō, -ōnis f.: account, reasoning
scrībō, -ere, scrīpsī, scrīptum: to write
sexus, -ūs m.: sex (biological)
silentium, -ī n.: silence
vetustus, -a, -um: old, ancient

Dē līberō arbitriō: *About free will;* implied reference back to Nogarola's argument about free will in 4.10
volō sexūs illīus dēceptiōnēs...silentiō praeterīre: *I want to pass by in silence the deceitfulness of that (the woman's) sex;* Foscarini uses *praeteritiō* to joke that he does not want to bring up women's inherent deceitfulness since he is writing to a woman
hōc vetustissimō verbō: *by this very old saying;* Boethius *Dē Cōns. Phil.* 3.5
firmētur ratiō: *let my reasoning be strengthened;* jussive subjunctive
efficācior...ad nocendum: *more harmful;* lit. "more effective for harming"
familiāris inimīcus: *friendly enemy;* an oxymoron that refers to an enemy who seems to (deceivingly) be a friend
prīma māter: *first mother;* i.e. Eve

quod nōndum nostrā ruīnā extīnctum est. Hoc maximam gravitātem peccātī significat. Nam velutī illae corporis aegritūdinēs sunt difficiliōrēs quae minus sānantur, sīc animī vitia.

5.12 Sī ego dīxī, nōn audiās; aspernēris et contemnās sī Augustīnus parī fastū conclūdit, "Ratiō quantō diūtius," etc.;

---

aegritūdō, -dinis f.: sickness

aspernor, aspernārī, aspernātus sum: to despise, scorn

Augustīnus, -ī m.: Augustine

conclūdō, -ere, conclūsī, conclūsum: to conclude

contemnō, -ere, contempsī, contemptum: to look down on

difficilis, -e: difficult

diū: (for) a long time

extinguō, -ere, extīnxī, extīnctum: to extinguish

fastus, -ūs m.: arrogance, pride

gravitās, -tātis f.: seriousness

minus: less (adv.)

nōndum: not yet

pār, paris: equal

quantō: (by) how much (adv.)

ratiō, -ōnis f.: reason, rationale

ruīna, -ae f.: destruction, collapse

sānō (1): to cure

significō (1): to indicate

velutī: just as

vitium, -ī n.: fault, defect

---

quod nōndum nostrā ruīnā extīnctum est: *conflagration which has not yet been extinguished by our collapse;* the idea refers to stopping the spread of fire in a city by making the building collapse on itself; Catiline reportedly said that he would put out the fire with his own collapse (Cic. *Mur.* 25.51; Sall. *Cat.* 31.9)

Sī ego...fatēbimur: a long sentence with three elements: Foscarini writes 1) do not believe me, 2) do not believe Augustine, Gregory, and the other authorities, 3) but let us read the Gospels and you will admit that I am right

Sī ego dīxī, nōn audiās: *If I have spoken, don't listen;* jussive subjunctive

aspernēris et contemnās: *despise it and scorn it;* jussive subjunctive; these verbs have three objects: Augustine's conclusion, Gregory's argument, and "etc." (presumably the other authorities cited by Foscarini)

parī fastū conclūdit: *concludes [that they sinned] with equal pride*

"Ratiō quantō diūtius": *"The rationale of how much longer";* referencing Gregory the Great's notion that the longer a person sinned, the more guilty they are (from 3.12 and 4.12)

Dē Parī aut Imparī Ēvae atque Ādae Peccātō 5.12

Passiōnis historiam legāmus et somnia uxōris, verba Pīlātī, manuum lōtiōnēs, iūdicandī fugam, et eum magis quam Iūdaeōs intellēxisse sententiam iniūstam fatēbimur. Ex quibus patet argūmentōrum nostrōrum vīrēs nōn dēficere.

argūmentum, -ī n.: argument
dēficiō, -ere, dēfēcī, dēfectum: to fail, to be lacking
fateor, fatērī, fassus sum: to confess
fuga, -ae f.: escape; avoidance
historia, -ae f.: history, narrative
iniūstus, -a, -um: unjust
intellegō, -ere, intellēxī, intellēctum: to understand
Iūdaeus, -ī m.: Judean, Jewish person; the Jews (pl.)

iūdicō (1): to judge
legō, -ere, lēgī, lēctum: to read
lōtiō, -ōnis f.: washing
passiō, -ōnis f.: suffering (of Christ)
pateō, -ēre, patuī, -: to stand open; to be clear
Pīlātus, -ī m.: Pilate
sententia, -ae f.: opinion; sentence (judicial)
somnium, -ī n.: dream
uxor, uxōris f.: wife

Passiōnis historiam legāmus: *Let us read the narrative of the Suffering;* that is, "the narrative of the suffering and death of Jesus"
verba Pīlātī: *the words of Pontius Pilate;* referring to Pilate's declaration that Jesus has done nothing wrong (Matthew 27:23, Mark 15:10–15, Luke 23:4, John 19:12)
somnia uxōris: *dreams of (Pilate's) wife;* Pilate's wife begs him to leave Jesus alone because of something she saw in a dream (Matthew 27:19)
manuum lōtiōnēs: *washing of hands;* Pilate washes his hands and says that Jesus's death was not his doing (Matthew 27:24)
iūdicandī fugam: *the avoidance of judging;* in the above accounts, Pilate turns over judgment to a crowd of Judeans
eum...intellēxisse sententiam iniūstam: *that he (Pilate)...understood the sentence to be unjust;* Foscarini is responding to Nogarola's argument from 4.13, but he seems to be rebutting a part of her idea that is not relevant to her argument
vīrēs: *strength;* from *vīs*
nōn dēficere: *is not lacking;* indirect statement set up by *patet*

5.13 Haec paucissimīs verbīs explicāvī, tum [215] quia papīrum trānsmissum iussus sum nōn excēdere, tum quia apud tē perītissimam loquor. Nōlō enim tantī itineris tibi, cui ex summā bonitāte omnia clārissima patent, dux esse. Vīvis profectō apud nōs in terrā velutī quaedam vītae caelestis imāgō.

---

bonitās, -tātis f.: goodness
caelestis, -e: celestial
excēdō, -ere, excessī, excessum: to exceed, go beyond
explicō (1): to explain
imāgō, -inis f.: image
iter, itineris n.: road; journey
labōrō (1): to work; suffer
loquor, loquī, locūtus sum: to speak
nōlō, nōlle, nōluī: to not want, not intend

obscūritās, -tātis f.: obscurity
papīrus, -ī m.: paper
pateō, patēre, patuī, -: to lie open
perītus, -a, -um: skilled, learned
profectō: really, actually
summus, -a, -um: highest
trānsmittō, -ere, trānsmisi, trānsmissum: to transmit, send
velutī: just as, as if
vitium, -ī n.: fault, defect

---

tum...tum: *not only...but also*
papīrum trānmissum iussus sum nōn excēdere: *I was ordered not to exceed the transmitted paper;* apparently referring to the guidelines Nogarola has given him
apud tē perītissimam loquor: *I am speaking with you (who are) most learned*
Nōlō enim tantī itineris tibi...dux esse: *I do not intend to be your leader on so great a journey;* literally "I do not want to be a leader to you of so great a journey"; Cicero writes a similar phrase in *Dē Ōrātōre* 1.203
clārissima patent: *lie open most clearly;* as usually, a nom. adj. comes out more smoothly in English as an adverb
velutī quaedam vītae caelestis imāgō: *as if a kind of image of heavenly life;* contemporary men frequently portrayed Nogarola as a kind of holy woman

Digitum, ut aiunt, ad fontēs intendī, et quamquam apud aliōs haec mea dicta obscūritātis vitiō labōrārent, sī apud tē clārissimam accēdent et priōribus tuīs ac meīs scrīptīs iungentur, apertissima fient, illūstrābuntur et radiābunt in tenebrīs. Atque ea sī ineptissima erunt, tuō studiō faciēs ingeniō, virtūte, glōriā tuā esse dignissima,

---

accēdō, -ere, accessī, accessum: to approach
aiō, -, -: to say
apertus, -a, -um: open, known
clārus, -a, -um: clear, brilliant
dictum, -ī n.: word
digitus, -ī m.: finger
dignus, -a, -um (+ abl.): worthy
fōns, fontis m.: fountain; source
glōria, -ae f.: glory
illūstrō (1): to illuminate
ineptus, -a, -um: foolish

ingenium, -ī n.: talent, genius
intendō, -ere, intendī, intentum: to hold out
iungō, -ere, iūnxī, iūnctum: to join
prior, prius: earlier (comp. adj.)
quamquam: although
radiō (1): to shine
scrīptum, -ī n.: writings
studium, -ī n.: skill
tenebrae, -ārum f.: darkness

Digitum...ad fontēs intendī: *I have held out (intendī) a finger (digitum) to the sources (ad fontēs);* a paraphrase of Cicero *Dē Ōrātōre* 1.203

mea dicta obscūritātis vitiō labōrārent: *my words may suffer from the defect of obscurity*

sī...accēdent: *if (my words) approach;* the implied subject is *mea dicta*

priōribus tuīs ac meīs scrīptīs: *to your earlier writings and my writings;* dative with *iungentur;* as in 5.1, Foscarini is referring to the idea that Nogarola will disseminate this work

ea sī ineptissima erunt: *if they are most foolish;* that is, if what Foscarini has written is most foolish

tuō studiō: *by your skill;* abl. of means with *faciēs*

faciēs ingeniō, virtūte, glōriā tuā esse dignissima: *you will make it to be most worthy of your talent, virtue, and glory; ingeniō, virtūte,* and *glōriā tuā* are abl. with *dignissima*

quae tē semper velutī mīlitēs tubārum clangōribus sīc sacrīs ēloquiīs ad nova proelia īnstrūctiōrem parātiōremque offers, contrā mē quidem, quī omnem meārum cōgitātiōnum summam legendō et eōdem, ut aiunt, spīritū scrībendō convertī ut ostendam [216] quod sentiō et dēfendam quod scrībis, licet plūribus negōtiōrum tempestātibus et flūctibus undique iacter. Valē.

---

aiō, -, -: to say

clangor, -ōris m.: blare, blast

cōgitātiō, -ōnis f.: thinking, thought

contrā (+ acc.): against

convertō, -ere, convertī, conversum: to turn; change direction in a march

dēfendō, -ere, dēfendī, dēfēnsum: to defend; defend against

ēloquium, -ī n.: eloquence; word

flūctus, -ūs m.: wave

iactō (1): to throw

īnstrūctus, -a, -um: learned, skilled

legō, -ere, lēgī, lēctum: to read

licet (+ subj.): although

negōtium, -ī n.: business

offerō, offerre, obtulī, oblātum: to offer

ostendō, -ere, ostendī, ostentum: to show, present

parātus, -a, -um: prepared

plūs, plūris: more (comp. adj.)

proelium, -ī n.: battle

sacer, -cra, -crum: holy, sacred

scrībō, -ere, scrīpsī, scrīptum: to write

sentiō, -īre, sēnsī, sēnsum: to perceive; think

spīritus, -ūs m.: spirit

summa, -ae f.: sum

tempestās, -tātis f.: storm

tuba, -ae f.: trumpet

undique: from every side

valē: goodbye

velutī: just as

---

quae tē...offers: *you who put yourself forward*

velutī mīlitēs tubārum clangōribus: *just as soldiers to the blares of trumpets;* implied that *tē...offers* also applies to this phrase; just as soldiers march forward to battles to the sound of trumpets, Nogarola marches forward to the sound of *sacrīs ēloquiīs*

quī...convertī: *I, who...have maneuvered;* this verb is often used for military maneuvers

plūribus negōtiōrum tempestātibus et flūctibus: *by many storms and waves of my responsibilities;* Foscarini is referring to his many responsibilities in public life as governor of Verona; *tempestātibus* and *flūctibus* are abl. of means

GLOSSARY

This glossary contains all the words that are not glossed in the running vocabulary. The words in this glossary are the 250 most commonly occurring words in Latin, drawn from the Dickinson College Commentaries Latin Core Vocabulary. We have also added the words "Adam" (Ādam, Ādae m.), "Eve" (Ēva, Ēvae f.), "woman" (mulier, mulieris f.) and "sin" (both as a verb, peccō (1), and a noun, peccātum, -ī n.), since these occur on almost every page of the text, and will likely be learned quickly by students.

ā/ab (+ abl.): by (agent); from
ac: and
accipiō, accipere, accēpī, acceptum: to take
ad (+ acc.): to, up to, towards; near to; in regards to
Ādam, Ādae m.: Adam (declined only in the genitive)
aliquis, aliquid: anyone/anything; someone/something
alius, alia, aliud: other, another
alter, altera, alterum: one (of two), the other, another
amīcus, amīca, amīcum: friendly; friend (as a substantive)
amō (1): to love
amor, amōris m.: love
animus, animī m.: mind; intellect; soul
annus, annī m.: year
apud (+ acc.): among; at the house of; in the presence of
at: but
atque: and; and moreover
audiō, audīre, audīvī, audītum: to hear, listen
aut: or; either...or (aut...aut)
autem: but (postpositive); however; moreover
bene: well
bonus, bona, bonum: good
caelum, caelī n.: heaven; the sky
capiō, capere, cēpī, captum: to take, seize; grasp
capitulum, capitulī n.: chapter
caput, capitis n.: head

castra, castrōrum n.: military camp, fortress (pl.)

causa, causae f.: cause; because of, for the sake of (causā + gen.)

cōgō, cōgere, coēgī, coāctum: to compel

cōnsilium, cōnsiliī n.: advice; planning; understanding, judgment

corpus, corporis n.: body

crēdō, crēdere, crēdidī, crēditum (+ dat.): believe; trust

cum (+ abl.): with

cum: when (+ indic.); since (+ subjunctive); although (+ subjunctive)

dē (+ abl.): down; from; about, concerning

dēbeō, dēbēre, dēbuī, dēbitum: to owe; ought (+ inf.)

deinde: then

deus, deī m.: god

dīcō, dīcere, dīxī, dictum: to say

diēs, diēī m.: day

dō, dare, dedī, datum: to give

dolor, dolōris m.: pain; grief

dominus, dominī m.: lord; master; owner

dūcō, dūcere, dūxī, ductum: to lead; think, consider

dum: while (+indic.); when (+ indic); until (+ subj.)

duo, duae, duo: two

dūrus, dūra, dūrum: hard; harsh

dux, ducis m.: leader, guide

ē/ex (+ abl.): out of; from

ego, meī, mihi, mē, mē: I, my, me (first person pron.)

enim: for, indeed (postpositive)

eō, īre, īvi(iī), itum: to go

ergō: therefore

et: and; even; also; even; both ... and (et ... et)

etiam: even; also, in addition

Ēva, Ēvae f.: Eve

faciō, facere, fēcī, factum: to do, make

ferō, ferre, tulī, lātum: to carry; take; endure

ferus, fera, ferum: wild

fidēs, fideī f.: faith

fīō, fierī, factus sum: to be made, be done; become; happen

genus, generis n.: origin; race, kind; type; family, descent

gerō, gerere, gessī, gestum: to carry; carry on; to indulge (*mōrem gerere*); to carry oneself, behave (*sē gerere*)

gravis, grave: heavy; serious; important

habeō, habēre, habuī, habitum: to have, hold, consider

hīc: here

hic, haec, hoc: this; these

homō, hominis m.: person; man

hostis, hostis m.: enemy

īdem, eadem, idem: the same (person or thing)

ignis, ignis m.: fire

ille, illa, illud: that; those

in (+ abl.): in, on

in (+ acc.): into; onto

inquam, -, -: to say (*inquit* is 3rd/sg.)

inter (+ acc.): between

ipse, ipsa, ipsum: himself/herself/itself

is, ea, id: he/she/it/they (third person pronoun)

iste, ista, istud: that, that of yours

ita: thus, so; in such a way; therefore

iubeō, iubēre, iussī, iussum: to order, command

labor, laboris m.: effort, labor; suffering, hardship

levis, leve: light, thin, trivial

līber, lībera, līberum: free

licet: it is permitted (+ inf.); although (+ subj.)

longus, longa, longum: long

magis: more; more-so (adv.)

magnus, magna, magnum: large, great; powerful; big

malus, mala, malum: bad, evil

manus, manūs f.: hand

mare, maris n.: sea

māter, mātris f.: mother

medius, media, medium: middle

mēns, mentis f.: mind; reason, judgement

meus, mea, meum: my

mīles, mīlitis m.: soldier

mittō, mittere, mīsī, missum: to send

modo: only (adv.)

modus, -ī m.: manner, way, method; measure, size; limit

mors, mortis f.: death

mōs, mōris m.: custom; character (pl.); to indulge (*mōrem gerere*)

moveō, movēre, mōvī, mōtum: to move, set in motion

mulier, mulieris f.: woman; wife

multus, multa, multum: much, many

nam: for; because

nātūra, nātūrae f.: nature

nātus, natī m.: son; child; children (pl.)

nē: not; that not (negation with subjunctives)

nec/neque: nor; and not

nihil n.: nothing

nisi: if not; except, unless

nōmen, nōminis n.: name

nōn: not; no

nōs, nostrī/nostrum, nōbīs, nōs, nōbīs: we, us

noster, nostra, nostrum: our

novus, nova, novum: new

nūllus, nūlla, nūllum: no, none, not any

nunc: now

oculus, oculī m.: eye

omnis, omne: each, every; all (pl.)

ōs, ōris n.: mouth

parēns, parentis: parent

parō, parāre, parāvī, parātum: to prepare; supply; produce

pars, partis f.: part; party, faction (sg. or pl.)

parum: too/very little, not enough (adv.)

parvus, parva, parvum: small, little

pater, patris m.: father

patior, patī, passus sum: to suffer; allow; undergo, endure

peccātum, -ī n.: sin

peccō, peccāre, peccāvī, peccātum: to sin

per (+ acc.): through (space); during (time); by, by means of

poena, -ae f.: penalty; punishment

pōnō, pōnere, posuī, positum: to put

populus, populī m.: people; nation

possum, posse, potuī: to be able, can

post (+ acc.): behind (space), after (time)
post: behind, afterwards, after (adv.)
prīmus, prīma, prīmum: first
prō (+ abl.): on behalf of; before; in instead of
puer, puerī m.: boy
pulcher, pulchra, pulchrum: beautiful; noble
putō, putāre, putāvī, putātum: to think
quam: than (after comparative); how
-que: and (enclitic)
quī, quae, quod: who, which, that (rel. pron.)
quia: since, because; that (starting a noun clause)
quīdam, quaedam, quoddam: a certain person/thing
quidem: indeed, certainly (postpositive)
quis, quid: who, what
quisquis, quidquid: whoever; whatever
quod: because; the fact that (starting a noun clause); that
quoque: too, also
relinquō, relinquere, relīquī, relictum: to leave behind, abandon
rēs, reī f.: thing
scelus, sceleris n.: crime; sin
sciō, scīre, scīvī, scītum: to know, understand
sed: but
semper: always
sequor, sequī, secūtus sum: to follow
sī: if
sīc: thus, so; as follows; in another way
sine (+ abl.): without
soleō, solēre, solitus sum: to become accustomed to, to usually do (something)
sōlum: alone (adv.)
sōlus, sōla, sōlum: alone; sole; only
spēs, speī f.: hope
stō, stāre, stetī, stātum: stand
sub (+ abl.): under
-, suī, sibi, sē, sē: himself, herself, itself, themselves (refl. pron.)
sum, esse, fuī, futūrum: to be; to exist
suus, sua, suum: his (own), her (own), its (own); (pl.) their (own)
tālis, tāle: such; of such a sort

tamen: yet, nevertheless

tantum: only (adv.)

tantus, tanta, tantum: of such size; so great, so much

tempus, temporis n.: time; season; age

teneō, tenēre, tenuī, tentum: to hold

terra, terrae f.: land, ground

timeō, timēre, timuī, -: to fear

tōtus, tōta, tōtum: whole, all

tū, tuī, tibi, tē, tē: you

tum: then, next; besides; at that time; both … and (tum … tum)

tunc: then, at that time

tuus, tua, tuum: your (sg.)

ubi: where; when

ūnus, ūna, ūnum: one

ut: to, in order to (+ subj.); how, when, as (+ indic.)

uter, utra, utrum: which (of two), either

vel: or; either … or (vel … vel)

veniō, venīre, vēnī, ventum: to come

verbum, verbī n.: word; a saying

via, viae f.: way; journey

videō, vidēre, vīdī, vīsum: to see; to seem (pass.)

vir, virī m.: man; husband

virtūs, virtūtis f.: excellence; strength; power

vīs, vīs f.: force; strength (pl.)

vīta, vītae f.: life

vīvō, vīvere, vīxī, vīctum: to live

vocō, vocāre, vocāvī, vocātum: to call, summon; name; call upon

volō, velle, voluī, -: to wish, want; be willing, will; intend

vōs, vestrī/vestrum, vōbīs, vōs, vōbīs: you (plural)

vōx, vōcis f.: voice

vultus, vultūs m.: face, expression